A Guide to Standard Grade French

by

T.G. McDonald, M.A.

ISBN 0 7169 3162 1
© *T.G. McDonald, 1991.*

REVISED EDITION 1998

ROBERT GIBSON · Publisher
17 Fitzroy Place, Glasgow, G3 7SF, Scotland, U.K.

CONTENTS

NOTE FROM THE AUTHOR

This book is intended as a basic guide to Standard Grade French for students and it is hoped they can use it independently to help in their preparation for the examination. It may be, however, that other interested parties such as teachers and parents may find it a useful source of information.

NOTE TO THE STUDENT

FAITES ATTENTION!

I sincerely hope that you find this book useful and wish you success in Standard Grade French. It is not however a passport to passing the exam, for only **you** can provide the hard work at home/school/college necessary to do well in any examination. If you are following a course at school or elsewhere it is most important that you put in your maximum effort there and use this publication to help you along the way. In fact the best preparation of all would be to emigrate to France for a year! As that will not be possible for most of you then hard work is the only alternative.

Alors! Bonne Chance!!

CHAPTER I

What is Standard Grade French?

In common with other Standard Grade subjects the examination is offered at three different levels — Foundation, General and Credit, Credit being the most difficult level. Within the examination there are three main elements, namely

> Speaking
> Listening
> Reading.

You will be awarded a grade for each of these elements according to how well you perform in each one.

The grading system is the same as for all Standard Grade examinations

> 1, 2 — Credit
> 3, 4 — General
> 5, 6 — Foundation.

However, because of the great importance attached to Speaking it is given "double weighting". You, therefore, count your Speaking award twice and add it to your awards for Listening and Reading, then divide by 4 to obtain your overall award. For example, if your grades were Speaking 2; Listening 3; Reading 1, your overall award would be

$$(2 + 2) + 3 + 1 = \frac{8}{4} = 2$$

There is a fourth element to the examination, namely Writing. I did not include it as a main part of the exam, because in fact it is an optional paper and the award gained does not influence your overall award in French, it will appear separately on your certificate. This part of the examination is offered only at General and Credit levels. Your teacher should discuss with you at what level you will be presented for Standard Grade French and whether or not you will sit the Writing option. It is normal practice to sit the examination at two levels viz., Credit + General + Foundation. Doing so both provides a "safety-net" in case you don't

4

do well in the higher of the two levels and also gives you the opportunity to see if you can achieve the higher level. Note that each level is assessed independently, so, for example, if you sat General and Credit and passed only the General level and failed the Credit, you would still be awarded a General award. On the other hand, you could in fact fail General, pass Credit and therefore be given the Credit level award. Still, enough of these confusing and boring statistics. If you are uncertain, discuss it with your teacher. Let us now move on to look at what you will be expected to learn in Standard Grade French.

ALORS, ALLONS-Y, AU TRAVAIL!!

What will I be learning in Standard Grade French?

Your teacher will have devised a two-year course to prepare you for Standard Grade French. He/she may choose to use a set course book or may base the course on a series of 'themes' (e.g. school, future career, etc.). Whichever method he/she chooses your teacher still has to make sure that the course meets the basic requirements set down by the Scottish Qualifications Authority (SQA). The SQA specifies 21 different Topic Areas, namely

1. Self.
2. Home.
3. Family / daily routine.
4. School.
5. Work.
6. Leisure.
7. Holidays and travel.
8. Environment, places and facilities.
9. Food and drink.
10. Goods and services.
11. Accidents and emergencies.
12. Events (past, present and future).
13. Clothes and fashion.
14. People.
15. Personal belongings / pets / money.
16. Places.
17. Immediate plans.
18. Time / dates
19. Weather.
20. Morals (happy, sad, etc.).
21. Physical state (hungry, thirsty, etc.).

It is important that you cover all of these topics before sitting the examination.

As your preparations will normally start two years before the examination it is essential that you keep good notes on the work you cover as few of us have a perfect memory. You should, in particular, keep a careful note of vocabulary — phrases and words — which you come across. It is a good idea to organise these into topic areas, perhaps using a loose-leaf binder so you can update regularly. Thus your section on "Self" will contain phrases such as

> *Je m'appelle . . .* — My name is . . .
> *J'ai . . . ans.* — I am . . . years old.
> *Dans ma famille nous sommes . . .* — In my family there are . . . of us.
> *Pendant mes loisirs je . . .* — In my free time I . . .

However, it is not simply enough to write down these phrases, you should regularly look over and learn them, as well as adding to them. It may be that your teacher will group some of these topics together to suit the particular course you are following. In any case, discuss with him/her how best to organise your notes. What else should you keep a note of? During your study of French you will be introduced to the rules of the language, often referred to as 'Grammar'! It is also important to keep a note of these rules as you go along. This will help to improve your competence in French **but** remember that while it is obviously better to say or write something accurately don't let a desire for accuracy stop you from having a go at saying something. It is more important to get the meaning through somehow, despite mistakes.

It is also a good idea to keep a record of some of the activities you have undertaken during your course to help you to revise for the examination. You should be set various tasks in French such as, "Book into an hotel and find out what facilities there are locally", or "Discuss your holiday plans with your French friend". These tasks will require you to use language from several topic areas. As I have said, keep a note of these tasks and revise them regularly. The next chapter will show how you might build up a unit of work and use the material contained in it to cope with Speaking tasks.

CHAPTER II

Sample Unit of Work

It will not be possible in this book to tell you **everything** you need to know for Standard Grade French. To do so it would have to run to several volumes. However, I will show you how you might organise one 'topic', the popular one of 'Leisure'. It will be organised in three parts.

1. Useful Language.
2. Associated Speaking Tasks.
3. Grammar.

Useful Language

1. *GENERAL VOCABULARY*

les passetemps	pastimes
les loisirs	leisure pursuits
le sport	sport
le football	football
le tennis	tennis
le golf	golf
l'équitation	horse riding
la natation	my friends listens to classical music
l'athlétisme	athletics
la gymnastique	gymnastics
le ski	skiing
le cinéma	cinema
la télé	television
la lecture	reading
la musique	music

2. *TO DO / TO PLAY*

FAIRE

faire du sport	to do a sport
je fais du sport	I do sport
je fais du judo	I do judo

il fait de l'athlétisme	he does athletics
Jean fait de la natation	John goes swimming

JOUER

jouer au foot	to play at football
je joue au foot	I play at football
Anne Marie joue au tennis	Anne Marie plays at tennis
mon père joue au golf	my father plays at golf
les français jouent á la pétanque ..	the French play bowls
je joue aux échecs	I play chess
je joue du piano	I play the piano
je joue de la guitarre	I play the guitar

PRATIQUER

pratiquer le golf	to play at golf
je pratique le golf	I play at golf
il pratique le volley	he plays at volley ball

3.   *GOING / WATCHING, etc.*

ALLER — TO GO

je vais au cinéma	I go to the cinema
je vais à une boum	I go to a party
elle va à la maison des jeunes	she goes to the youth club
on va aux concerts	we go to concerts

REGARDER — TO WATCH

je regarde la télé	I watch T.V.
je regarde les feuilletons	I watch "soaps"
il regarde les émissions de sport ...	he watches sports programmes
ma mère regarde les documentaries	my mother watches documentaries

ÉCOUTER — TO LISTEN TO

j'écoute des disques	I listen to records
j'écoute la radio	I listen to radio
j'écoute la musique pop	I listen to pop music
mon ami écoute la musique classique	my friend listens to classical music

4. LIKING / NOT LIKING / PREFERRING, etc.

AIMER — TO LIKE

j'aime	I like
j'aime bien / beaucoup	I like . . . a lot
j'aime surtout	I especially like
il aime	he likes
on aime bien	we like . . . a lot
je n'aime pas	I don't like
je n'aime pas tellement	I don't like . . . very much
je n'aime pas du tout	I don't like . . . at all

ADORER — TO LOVE / DÉTESTER — TO HATE / PRÉFÉRER — TO PREFER

j'adore	I love
on adore	we love
je déteste	I hate
Michel déteste	Michael hates
je préfère	I prefer

Any of the above phrases for liking / not liking, etc., can be combined as follows:

A   With the name of the activity, e.g.

j'aime le golf	I like golf
je n'aime pas tellement le sport	I don't like sport very much
il aime bien la lecture	he likes reading a lot
Louise adore la musique	Louise loves music
je n'aime pas du tout les feuilletons	I don't like "soaps" at all
on déteste la musique classique	we hate classical music
je préfère la natation	I prefer swimming

B   With a phrase containing the infinitive of a verb.

e.g. *je n'aime pas . . .*; *j'aime bien . . .*; *il adore . . .*, etc.

aller à la disco	going to the disco
aller au cinéma	going to the cinema
jouer au foot	playing at football
écouter les disques de U.2.	listening to U.2. records
sortie avec mes copains	going out with my friends
rester à la maison	to stay at home
lire des romans	to read novels

9

5. *EXPRESSING AN OPINION*

This can of course be done by using expressions of liking / not liking, etc., but here are some other ways.

c'est	it is
ce n'est pas	it is not
je pense que c'est	I think it is
je trouve que c'est	I think it is
à mon avis c'est	in my opinion it is
bien	good
formidable	great
super	super
génial / sensas / extra	brilliant
moche	terrible
ennuyeux	boring
intéressant	interesting

e.g. *Le football? Je trouve que c'est ennuyeux.*
La musique pop? A mon avis, c'est super!
Regarder la télè? Moi, je pense que ce n'est pas intéressant.

6. *SAYING WHEN*

pendant mon temps libre	during my free time
pendant mes heures de loisir	during my free time
quand j'ai un moment de libre	when I have a free moment
normalement	normally, usually
tous les jours	every day
tous les soirs	every evening
pendant le weekend	at the weekend
pendant la semaine	during the week
le samedi	on Saturdays
de temps en temps	from time to time
quelquefois	sometimes
parfois	sometimes
pendant les vacances	during the holidays
quand je suis seul	when I am alone
quand je suis chez moi	when I am at home
quand je sors avec la bande	when I go out with my pals

7. *SAYING FOR HOW LONG*

depuis cinq ans . . . . for five years
depuis un mois . . . . for one month

e.g. *je fais du judo depuis six mois*
     I have been doing judo for six months

8. *OTHER USEFUL PHRASES*

Passer le temps à faire quelquechose
to spend your time doing something.

e.g. *je passe mon temps libre à écouter mes disques*
     I spend my free time listening to my records

Pendant l'heure du déjeuner j'aime passer le temps à bavarder avec mes amis.
During lunch break I like spending the time chatting with my friends.

s'intéresser à (faire quelquechose)
to be interested in (doing something)

e.g. *Je m'intéresse à la lecture.*
     I'm interested in reading.

     Il s'intéresse à colectionner des timbres.
     He's interested in collecting stamps.

mon passetemps favori c'est . . .	my favourite pastime is . . .
mon sport préféré c'est . . .	my favourite sport is . . .
mon groupe favori c'est . . .	my favourite group is . . .

9. *ASKING QUESTIONS*

In addition to talking about yourself and others you may have to find out from someone else what their pastimes are, what they like, etc. To do so you will obviously have to ask questions such as

Tu aimes?	Do you like?
Vous aimez?	Do you like?
Tu aimes aller au cinéma?	Do you like going to the cinema?
Tu regardes la télé	Do you watch television
Est-ce que vous jouez au golf?	Do you play at golf?

11

Est-ce que to préfères la musique pop ou la musique classique?
Do you prefer pop or classical music?

Comment passes-tu ton temps libre?	How do you spend your free time?
Allez-vous au café?	Do you go to the café?
Qu'est-ce tu penses du football? . . .	What do you think of football?
Qu'est-ce que vous pensez des feuilletons?	What do you think of "soaps"?
Tu t'intérèsse aux échecs?	Are you interested in chess?
Qu'est-ce que tu fais au weekend? . .	What do you do at weekends?
Qu'est-ce que vous faites chez vous?	What do you do at home?
Quel est ton passetemps favori?	What's your favourite pastime?
Quel est votre disque préféré	What's your favourite record?

The form of the questions will vary according to whether you are talking to a friend, an older person you don't know very well or perhaps more than one person. This will be explained more fully in the grammar section.

There now follow some Speaking tasks for which you could use the language above.

Associated Speaking Tasks

1. Prepare a short talk about your pastimes. This could be delivered to your classmates or recorded to send to a penpal. It should last at least 1 minute.

    It might go something like this.

    > *Mes passetemps? Alors, je suis très sportif. J'aime bien faire du sport. Je joue au foot et je fais du tennis, mais je n'aime pas tellement le rugby, je trouve que c'est violent. Le soir j'adore sortir avec mes copains. Normalment on va à la maison des jeunes et on écoute des disques et on bavarde. C'est génial. Je m'intérèsse à la lecture et je préfère les romans policiers. Je n'aime pas tellement regarder la télé, je pense que c'est ennuyeux. Moi, je préfère passer les temps à lire ou à écouter des disques dans ma chambre. Pendant le weekend j'adore aller au cinéma. J'aime bien les films avec beaucoup d'action. En hiver je fais du ski. A mon avis c'est très difficile mais c'est sensas! Je fais du ski depuis deux ans. Je trouve que la musique est formidable, surtout la musique pop. Je ne sais pas jouer d'un instrument mais mon frère, il joue de la guitarre.*

Now try making up a similar talk about yourself using as wide a range of phrases as possible. Try not to use the verb 'aimer' too often! When you give this kind of talk in class you may be allowed only a few notes, so try doing it that way first by writing down a few headings as follows.

Les Passetemps

Sportif.
Foot / tennis / rugby.
Le soir — maison des jeunes — copains.
Lecture — romans policiers.
Télé — préfère disques.
Cinéma — film d'action.
Le ski — deux ans — difficile.
La musique — frère.

This exercise could also be treated as a written one and developed into a written account of your pastimes, in a letter for example. Try it!!

2. Interview your teacher or perhaps the French assistant about his/her hobbies and pastimes.

You might wish to make a list of possible questions as follows.

Qu'est-ce que vous aimez faire?
Pendant vos loisirs.
Le soir / au weekend.
Vous aimez (le ski)?
Vous êtes sportif?
Vous faites (du sport)?
Vous jouez à
Vous jouez de
Vous aimez aller (au cinéma)?
Vous pratiquez (un sport)?
Qu'est-ce que vous pensez de . . .
Vous vous intérèssez à . . .
Depuis combien de temps est-ce que vous jouez au golf?
Quel est votre groups / film, etc. préféré?

You should be prepared to ask some follow-up questions too.

3. Imagine you are a famous film / pop star. Tell someone else all about your leisure time. This could be similar to Task 1 but it will give you a chance to use your imagination.

Grammar

There are several main grammar points involved in a unit like this. As I have said before, a knowledge of these rules of language will help you to develop your language ability beyond mere set phrases and to adapt it to suit many situations. Here are some of the grammar points involved.

1. *The Verbs*

   The following verbs are those most commonly used in this unit. Here is the present tense of each one.

   ### Aimer — *to like*

j'aime	— I like	*nous aimons*	— we like
tu aimes	— you like	*vous aimez*	— you like
il / elle aime	— he / she likes	*ils aiment*	— they like
on aime	— one likes	*elles aiment*	— they like
	— we like		

   ### Faire — *to do/make*

je fais	— I do	*nous faisons*	— we do
tu fais	— you do	*vous faites*	— you do
il / elle fait	— he / she does	*ils font*	— they do
on fait	— one does	*elles font*	— they do
	— we do		

   ### Aller — *to go*

je vais	— I go	*nous allons*	— we go
tu vas	— you go	*vous allez*	— you go
il / elle va	— he / she goes	*ils vont*	— they go
on va	— one goes	*elles vont*	— they go
	— we go		

   ### Jouer — *to play*

je joue	— I play	*nous jouons*	— we play
tu joues	— you play	*vous jouez*	— you play
il / elle joue	— he / she plays	*ils jouent*	— they play
on joue	— one plays	*elles jouent*	— they play
	— we play		

   N.B.   JOUER is a regular "er" verb. Other verbs you have found within this unit behave the same way, e.g. pratiquer, adorer, regarder.

A knowledge of these verbs will help you to adapt the phrases you have learned. For example, you could change *j'aime la lecture* (I like reading) to *ils aiment la lecture* (they like reading) or *je vais au cinéma* (I go to the cinema) to *il va au cinéma* (he goes to the cinema).

GOT THE IDEA??

2. *Use of the Definite Article (THE)*

In English we say "I like football", "I love horse riding", "I prefer pop music" and so on. However, if you examine the French phrases "*j'aime le football*", "*j'adore l'équitation*" and "*je préfère la musique pop*" you should spot that the word for the (*le, la, l', les*) is used. This is the case after any verb of liking / preferring, etc.

How would you say to following?
   (i)   I like television.
   (ii) I hate golf.
   (iii) He doesn't like reading very much.

3. *To Play Something (when using jouer)*

   (a)   To play sport or game you use "*jouer à*" + the sport or game, e.g.

> *je joue au football*
> *il joue aux echecs.*

   (Remember "*a + le*" becomes "*au*" and "*a + les*" becomes "*aux*".)

   (b)   To play an instrument you use "*jouer de*" + the instrument, e.g.

> *je joue du piano*
> *il joue de la guitarre.*

   (Remember "*de + le*" becomes "*du*".)

4. *Saying for How Long*

To say for example
> I have been golfing for 5 years you would say
> "*je joue au golf depuis 5 ans*".

Notice that the construction is
Present tense of verb + *depuis* + time
e.g. *je fais du ski depuis 6 mois*
> I have been skiing for 6 months
> *je joue de la guitarre depuis 2 ans*
> I have been playing the guitar for 2 years.

15

5. *French for 'YOU'*

Remember there are two different ways of saying 'you' in French.

(i)   *TU* — You use this when talking to one person who is a young person, a friend or a member of your family.

(ii) *VOUS* — You use this always when talking to more than one person or when talking to one person who is an adult unknown to you or to whom you have to be polite such as a shopkeeper, policeman, etc.

This is important especially when asking questions and will decide which part of the verb you use. Look back at the questions in this unit and try changing them to the alternative form.

As I have said before it is important not to neglect the rules of the language but please remember that it is better to get the message through with mistakes than not to get it through at all.

CHAPTER III

SPEAKING

As I mentioned earlier in Chapter I, Speaking forms 50% of your overall award at Standard Grade. This shows the great importance attached to the skill of Speaking when learning a language. Just think how much time you spend speaking your own native language! The ability to speak the language is by far the most valuable skill and the one you are most likely to make use of, whether in your future career or on holiday. It is vital then to develop this skill by making the most of every opportunity which you have to speak French. Don't be put off by the fear of making mistakes. The more you try to speak French, the greater your confidence will become and you will find that accuracy will improve too. Remember that few people speak their own language absolutely perfectly. The most important thing is not to clam up but to have a go at it!

How is Speaking Assessed?

Your Speaking performance is in fact assessed internally by the school or institution you attend.

During the final year of your Standard Grade course your teacher will try to gain an impression of how well you can speak French in class. He/She will listen to you on several occasions throughout the year while you are doing a variety of Speaking Activities. It is not really possible to explain what these activities will be or how your teacher will assess them exactly as institutions use many different systems and none is specified by The Scottish Qualifications Authority. The best advice I can give you is to ask your teacher to explain his/her system to you and to try to speak French as often as possible and to put in as much effort as possible, bearing in mind what has already been said about having a go and not being afraid of how you sound or the mistakes you may make. Although your teacher will use his/her own system to assess your performance he/she will be looking for some or all of the following points:

1.   Making yourself understood.
2.   Accent, intonation.
3.   Accuracy.
4.   How well you understand.
5.   Can you go beyond minimum answers.

6. Can you ask for help.
7. Do you use a variety of language.

Overall your teacher should be trying to establish your normal performance when speaking French in the classroom.

As I have said before, it is up to each centre to decide what kinds of activity will be used for assessing your speaking performance. However, here is a list of some possible activities you may be faced with.

1. Speaking French in the classroom.
2. Warming up at the beginning of class.
   (What did you do last night? / Did you see that film? / Where are you going this weekend?)
3. A transactional task, i.e. buying something, asking for directions, booking in.
4. Interviewing an adult (e.g. about pastimes).
5. Interviewing a classmate (e.g. about future plans).
6. A prepared talk using notes (e.g. about your family).
7. An unprepared talk.
8. A group discussion.
9. A report on something you have listened to or read.
10. Taking part in a game.
11. A short playlet.

The above list by no means contains all possible kinds of Activity. The important thing for you is to make sure you make the most of every opportunity you have to speak French.

Moderation

In order to check on the accuracy of the speaking marks from a centre, the Scottish Qualifications Authority (SQA) carries out moderation procedures. This means that each centre is visited regularly by an external examiner who will sit in and observe a speaking test being taken by a number of candidates. The test is set by the SQA and is assessed by the teacher and examiner using guidelines called Grade Related Criteria. These guidelines are fairly complex but I will highlight below some of the things your teacher will be looking for.

1. How well you understand what he / she says to you. How simple or complicated he/she can make his / her language and how quickly he/she can speak. How much help does he / she have to provide.

18

2. Do you give only minimal responses or do you try to go beyond them and take the initiative? (For cxample, do you settle for *oui* or *non* responses or do you give morc information?)

3. How well you make yourself understood.

4. The kind of language you use. For example do you 'play safe' and use only very simple language to avoid making mistakes, or do you try to go beyond that and use a wider variety of phrases and expressions?

5. The accuracy of your language.

6. What your language sounds like — this includes accent, amount of hesitation, use of English.

In short, your teacher will be trying to get an overall impression of your ability to speak French in this Test situation.

N.B. Although you may not be chosen for moderation, it is fairly common practice for centres to use this exercise as a final speaking test for candidates.

You will normally be given the test paper homc to prepare beforehand. This is a chance not to be wasted.

The paper you arc givcn home will contain

1. Details of the situation, i.e. where it is taking place and what role your teacher will play. (N.B. You will normally play *yourself*.)

2. The three Areas of the situation, i.e. what you have to do and talk about.

3. Some suggestions as to what to talk about.

On the day of the test thc paper you have in front of you will be similar to the one explained above, except that it will not contain any suggestions, just the three Areas.

Being able to take the test home to prepare probably seems like a great idea and you may think it makes it easy. That is not quite the case. The purpose of doing so allows you to come into the exam with something to say and hopefully that should give you a little confidence so you don't arrive shaking like a jelly!

Examine the test carefully to discover what topics you have to talk about and therefore what language you will have to use. Let us look at a sample test and try some preparation.

This sample test provides five areas rather than the three required in the SQA test. This is designed to provide you with a wider range of the kind of situations you might expect to face.

The situation you have to imagine is:

> You are spending your summer holidays in France camping with your family. You arrive at a camp-site and you go into the office to book in. You talk to the owner.

AREA 1: Book into the camp-site

Be prepared to give details of how many people there are, how long you want to stay for, etc.

AREA 2: Find out about the facilities on the site

Be prepared to ask what there is to do, where things are, how much they cost and so on.

AREA 3: You notice a poster offering activities for young people — find out about it

Be prepared to find out what is on offer and discuss what you like doing

AREA 4: Talk about your holiday so far

Be prepared to say where you have been, what you did, what you thought of it, etc.

AREA 5: The owner says he / she has a 15 year old son who could show you around. Find out about him and arrange to meet later.

Be prepared to find out his name and interests and arrange where and when to meet.

Remember that on the day of the examination your paper will only show the details in the boxes above.

Preparation

Consider each area and list the kind of language you might use. Try to anticipate questions you might be asked and questions you could ask yourself and look up your notebook to help you. Try going through it with a friend or member of your family. Here is how you might make some notes by way of preparation.

AREA 1

Bonjour Monsieur / Madame. — Hello, Sir / Madam.
Avez vous un emplacement libre? — Do you have a spare pitch?
C'est pour ... personnes. — It's for ... people.
C'est pour ... nuits. — It's for ... nights.
On préfère un emplacement près des douches.—
We'd like a pitch near the showers.
C'est combien par nuit? — How much is it per night?
Nous avons une tente / caravane. — We have a tent / caravan.

AREA 2

Qu'est-ce qu'il y a? — What is there?
Il y a un magasin? (etc.) — Is there a shop? (etc.)
Où est le restaurant? (etc.) — Where is the restaurant? (etc.)
Qu'est-ce qu'on peut faire? — What can one do?
On peut ... jouer au foot? (etc.) — Can you ... play at football? (etc.)
Ça commence à quelle heure? — What time does it begin?
Ça coute combien? — How much is it?

AREA 3

(There may be some overlap with AREA 2.)
Qu'est-ce qu'il ya à faire pour les jeunes?—
What is there for young people to do?
Moi, j'aime ... — Me, I like ...
Moi je m'intérèsse à ... — I'm interested in ...
Je suds ... sportif. — I am sporty.
Ça m'attire — That appeals to me.
Ça ne me dit pas grande chose. — I don't really fancy that.

21

On est arrivés en France (le 5 juillet). — We arrived in France (on 5th July.)
On a passé 3 jours en Normandie. — We spent 3 days in Normandy.
Il a fait beau / du soleil. — The weather was nice / sunny.
On a visité un château. — We visited a castle.
(l'ai visité . . .)   — (I visited . . .)
J'ai acheté des souvenirs. — I bought some souvenirs
On est allés (Je suis allé) à Bayeux. — We (I) went to Bayeux.
On a vu la cathédrale. — We saw the cathedral.
C'était . . . formidable / super. — It was brilliant / great.
Je l'ai trouvé . . . ennuyeux. — I found it . . . boring".

Comment s'appelle-t-il? — What's his name?
Il a quel âge? — What's his age?
Qu'est-ce qu'il aime faire? — What does he like doing?
Quels sont ses passetemps favoris? — What are his favourite pastimes?
Il est. . . sportif? — Is he sporty?
Où est-ce qu'on se rencontre? — Where shall we meet?
A quelle heure? — At what time?

This language will help you to say something about each area and give you some confidence. Of course, simply memorising phrases like these won't guarantee that you will do well. You have to take part in a conversation with your teacher and that obviously means listening carefully to what he/she has to say and ask and respond to it. Your teacher will also want to see if you can go beyond learned phrases. However it is safe to say that your preparation will prove very valuable indeed. Do you see how very important it will be to have kept a good note of useful language? Make sure you do so! Did you spot how several topics were included, for example, self, holidays, travel, places, facilities, plans and so on.

Preparation for Moderation Test or Final Speaking Assessment

Here is a short summary of how you should prepare.

1.   Make sure you are present the day the test is given out.

2. Read through all the instructions very carefully. If there is anything you do not understand ask your teacher.

3. Ask your teacher's advice on how to prepare.

4. At home. Go through the test and try to work out what will be expected of you. Ask an adult to help you, if possible. You might even try it with a class friend.

5. For each of the five areas try to identify what questions you may have to ask and answer, and any other language you might require to take part.

6. Look up your notebook and jot down words and phrases you think will be useful for each area. Look up any others you are not sure of.

7. Try out the test with someone else who speaks French, perhaps even a classmate. Failing that, try talking to yourself!

8. On the day of the test make sure you turn up in plenty of time.

9. Don't panic!! Try to relax as much as possible. Your teacher knows you will be feeling nervous and will help you along.

10. **Listen** extremely carefully and ask (in French) for repetition or clarification of anything you don't understand, e.g.

    Pardon, voulez-vous répéter s'il vous plait?
    (Sorry, could you repeat that please?)

    Je ne comprends pas (I don't understand.)

    Qu'est-ce que ça veut dire? (What does that mean?)

    Do not use a phrase like *comment dit-on en français?*—this is acceptable in the normal classroom but is not appropriate in a test situation.

11. **Pause for thought.** There are also some simple strategies to give you time to think. Using them will also make your conversation sound more natural. Try to use some of the following

eh bien — well	*voyons* — let's see
alors — well	*tu vois* — you see
euh . . . qu'est-ce que j'allais dire? — . . . what was I going to say?	

12. Look at your teacher throughout the test. Make 'eye contact'.

13. Sit up and smile!

14. Try not to limit yourself to very short answers — try to go beyond them as far as possible and don't be put off by mistakes.

15. Take the initiative. You are not there to be interrogated by the teacher. Try to say as much as you can. This is your chance to show off what you can do in French. You should try to dominate the conversation as much as possible.

16. If the test doesn't seem to be following the 5 areas exactly, don't worry. You teacher is free to develop it in a way which suits you.

BONNE CHANCE!

CHAPTER IV

LISTENING

It is really beyond the scope of this little book to provide a great deal of help in the Listening section of the examination. As previously stated you will be presented for Listening at probably two of the levels, Foundation, General or Credit. Obviously the level of difficulty of the Listening tasks will increase the higher the grade you take. Here is a brief explanation of what to expect at each of the levers.

1. *Foundation*

    Items will range from simple words or phrases to a few connected sentences. The language used will be very straightforward and will be spoken clearly and slowly.

2. *General*

    Items will consist of short conversations or passages. The language used will be more difficult and should usually be spoken at near normal speed.

3. *Credit*

    Items will consist of conversation and passages probably longer than at General level and using more complex language and ideas. It will be spoken at near normal speed.

Advice

(i) Try to listen to spoken French as often as possible. You should have plenty of opportunities in class to do so but you could also perhaps ask your teacher to provide you with some Listening material to listen to at home. The more you listen to French the more you will understand it.

(ii) During the examination you will hear each item twice. Make sure you have studied the question beforehand and are sure what information you are looking for. At General and Credit level you may have to extract the relevant details from the conversation or passage.

25

(iii) **Concentrate.** It is extremely important when listening that you do concentrate as hard as possible. It is easy to find yourself distracted by some other noise, someone moving, something you see through the window and so on. Try looking down at your paper or even closing your eyes to help you to concentrate.

It is very important that you work hard at improving your listening skills not just because understanding the spoken word is a vital skill, but is also equally vital when taking part in a conversation in French, including the Final Proficiency Test.

CHAPTER V

WRITING

Writing in Standard Grade French

In Chapter I of this book you were told that the Writing paper is an optional one, and you were only offered it at General and Credit levels. It is up to you and your teacher to decide whether you should tackle the Writing paper, and if so at what level. Remember that it will **not** be taken into account in your overall award: that is decided by your performance in Speaking, Listening and Reading. If you achieve an award in Writing it will appear separately on the certificate you receive. However, you have nothing to lose by having a go at Writing and those of you who intend to continue your study of French beyond Standard Grade would be well advised to do so.

What will you be asked to do in the Writing paper of the Standard Grade examination? Let us take a look at what will be expected of you.

General Level

> You will be expected to do several tasks ranging from a few sentences about yourself, writing a short message or perhaps sending a note to someone. Your performance will be judged on your ability to communicate the information. This may be done despite mistakes in your language. Here are some examples of what to expect.
>
> (i) Write **three** sentences about your family.
>
> (ii) Write **four** sentences about your house.
>
> (iii) You decide to go to the cinema. Leave a note for your friend saying where you have gone, when the film starts and give directions how to get there.
>
> (iv) Send a postcard to your penpal when you arrive home saying how much you enjoyed your stay, what the journey was like and what you did during it.

The first two are fairly simple tasks requiring simple language. Do not make it complicated.

Here is how you might tackle them..

(i) *J'ai deux frères.*
Je n'ai pas de soeur.
Mon père s'appelle John.

(ii) *J'habite une maison.*
C'est grande.
Il y a un jardin.

(iii)   *Cher Jean,*

Je suis allé au cinéma. Le film commence à 8 heures. Le cinéma est dans la Rue Principale à côté du supermarché "Monoprix".

Mark.

OR

Jeanne,

Au ciné. Film commence à 8 heures. Tourne à gauche, va tout droit et c'est à gauche.

Marie.

N.B. It is important to provide the three pieces of information required, namely

(a)   Where you have gone.
(b)   When the film starts.
(c)   How to get there.

Don't put in any extra information and don't make it more complicated than necessary, especially the directions. Remember it is a short note you are leaving and not a letter so your language can consist of simple short phrases. You are attempting to communicate the information as simply as possible, not write a long essay about it!

(iv)

```
Cher Jeanne,

    Me voici chez moi.
    Merci beaucoup. Tout était
    formidable. Voyage très long
    et ennuyeux.

    J'ai lu et écouté mon
    "Walkman".

                        Lesley
```

Again it is important to convey the information requested in a simple format. As in English, when you write a note or a postcard in French you can use short phrases and miss out certain words. For example, in the postcard above we said *"Voyage très long et ennuyeux."* instead of *"Le voyage était très long et ennuyeux."* This shortened version is perfectly acceptable and in fact is better when writing a postcard.

Some more examples of Writing at General Level will be found later in this book.

Credit Level

The Writing task at Credit level is quite different from those found at General level. Normally you will be asked to write about 200 words on a topic which will be introduced to you by asking you to read a passage or several short statements about that topic. The topic should be something you are familiar with, for example

       school
       pocket money
       leisure pursuits
       television, etc.

The topic will normally be introduced to you by some stimulus material. Normally this will take the form of short passages on the same topic. These are intended to be helpful by presenting you with some opinions and ideas on the topic you are asked to write about. The language used should also prove useful. Don't worry if you don't understand all of the passages. You don't have to use the ideas and language contained in them. They are simply designed to help you get started on your own essay.

You will normally be asked to write down your ideas, views, opinions on the topic concerned, so it is worthwhile learning phrases in French which will help you to express your thoughts. Here are some you might make use of.

These phrases could also prove useful, of course, for your speaking activities and test.

> *j'aime* — I like
> *j'aime bien* — I like . . . a lot
> *j'aime beaucoup* — I like . . . very much
> *j'adore* — I love
> *je préfère* — I prefer
> *je détèste* — I hate
> *je trouve que* — I find that
> *je pense que* — I think that
> *je pense que oui* — I think so
> *je pense que non* — I don't think so
> *j'estime que* — I think that
> *je suppose que* — I suppose that
> *à mon avis* — in my opinion
> *il me semble que . . .* — it seems to me that . . .
> *je suis d'accord* — I agree
> *je ne suis pas d'accord* — I don't agree
> *cette idée ne me plait pas tellement* — I don't think much of that idea
> *Tout d'abord je veux dire que* — First of all, I would like to say that
> *Je fais partie de ceux qui pensent que* —
>> I am one of those who think that
> *je suis persuadé que* — I am convinced that
> *il y a des gens qui disent que . . .* — Some people think that . . .

il vaudrait mieux . . . — it would be better to
en revanche — on the other hand
au contraire — on the contrary
en conclusion — in conclusion
il y a des avantages — there are advantages
il y a des inconvénients — there are disadvantages
bref — in short
en fin de compte — all things considered.

Before you start writing your essay take time to do some planning. I would advise the following system.

1. Look through the stimulus passages.
2. Note down the main ideas you find.
3. Note down any language you think would be useful.
4. Jot down your own ideas on the subject.
5. Decide which ideas you wish to incorporate into your essay and in which order. Write down this plan.
6. Use your dictionary to check on any words or phrases you are not sure about.
7. Write your essay using your plan to guide you.
8. Be careful not to simply copy large chunks from the stimulus.

Here is a sample question with a step by step guide to producing an essay. Read the passages below. Three young French people give their views on school uniforms.

L'UNIFORME

MARIE:
Chez nous, en France, on ne porte pas l'uniforme. On porte ce qu'on veut. Moi j'aime bien être confortable donc je mets un jean et un vieux pull. Porter l'uniforme? Bof, je n'aimerais porter les mêmes vêtements que tous les autres.

XAVIER:
Moi j'ai passé une année dans un collège en Angleterre où on a été obligé de porter l'uniforme — pantalon bleue, chemise blanche et même une cravate!! Au début je l'ai trouvé un peu bizarre et inconfortable, surtout quand il a fait chaud. Mais, en revanche, je crois que il y a un avantage . . . c'est que tout le monde — riche ou pauvre — est égal.

31

CLAIRE:

L'uniforme? Alors, à mon avis c'est ridicule. À l'àge de 15 ans on a sûrement le droit de choisir ce qu'on porte. Moi, je ne me sentirais pas à l'aise dans une uniforme! J'aime mieux êtrer à la mode.

The passages above introduce you to the topic of school uniforms and should help you to express your own thoughts.

What ideas can you take from them?

You might note the following.

> *On ne porte pas l'uniforme en France*
> *être confortable*
> *porter les mêmes vêtements que les autres*
> *l'uniforme est bizarre et inconfortable*
> *quand il a fait chaud*
> *on est égal*
> *on à le droit de choisir.*

WHAT USEFUL LANGUAGE IS THERE?

You might note the following.

> *chez nous*
> *on porte / on ne porte pas*
> *je mets*
> *être obligé de*
> *en revanche*
> *à l'age de 15 ans*
> *être à la môde*
> *aimer mieux.*

WHAT ARE YOUR OWN IDEAS?

You might note the following.

> *l'uniforme de mon collège*
> *moi, je porte . . .*
> *je trouve que c'est inconfortable*
> *je préfère porter un jean et un pull*
> *les avantages —   tout le monde égal*
> *discipline*
> *les profs, les parents*

les inconvénients — au contraire / les jeunes
inconfortable s'il fait chaud
ce n'est pas à la môde
porter les mêmes vêtements que les autres
mon opinion — je ne suis pas d'accord
à l'âge de 15 ans on a le droit de porter ce qu'on veut
plus à l'aise
en France on n'est pas obligé ... pourquoi en Ecosse?

The plan on pages 32 and 33 could form the basis for the following essay.

L'uniforme au collège. Alors, tout d'abord je veux dire qu à mon collège il faut porter l'uniforme. On porte une jupe ou un pantalon noir, chemise gris et une cravate. Moi je porte l'uniforme mais je la déteste. Je trouve que c'est inconfortable. Je préfère porter un jean et un pull.

Pourquoi porter l'uniforme? Je suppose qu'il y a des avantages. Il y a des gens (les profs et les parents) qui pensent que c'est une bonne idée. Bof! On dit que c'est bon pour la discipline et que tout le monde est égal.

Au contraire, les jeunes n'aiment pas porter l'uniforme parce que ce n'est pas à la mode et ils n'aiment pas porter les mêmes vêtements que les autres. En plus, c'est très inconfortable, surtout quand il fait chaud.

Moi, je suis d'accord avec les jeunes. Je suis persuadé que, à l'âge de 15 ans, j'ai le droit de porter ce que je veux. Je préfererais mettre mon jean et mon pull pour aller au collège. Je pense que je me sentirais plus à l'aise pendant les cours. En France on n'est pas obligé de porter l'uniforme. On porte ce qu'on veut. Eh bien, pourquoi pas ici en Ecosse? Ce n'est pas juste!

I don't, of course, expect you to be able to produce an essay of the standard shown above. However, if you do enough preparation and do some careful planning, you can certainly do well in Credit Writing in French.

CHAPTER VI

THE USE OF THE DICTIONARY

During the tests of Reading and Writing you will have the company of a very valuable friend — your dictionary! It is important that you take advantage of this and use it properly. Beware — misuse of a dictionary can seriously damage your French! In this section of the book I will give you some advice on how to make proper use of it.

1. **Finding your way around**

   During the examination you will make use of your dictionary but it is important not to waste too much time. The following points should help you to avoid that.

   (i) Don't look up every single word. Try to focus on those you think are important to the meaning of the passage and check on them if necessary.

   (ii) Remember that dictionaries are split into two sections
   - *(a)* French → English,
   - *(b)* English → French.

   Don't confuse the two sections. You could perhaps put in a marker or a spare pen to divide the different sections.

   (iii) Remember that words are entered in alphabetical order.

   (iv) At the top of each page there will be words in larger, bolder type to help you find the correct page before you have to start searching through the smaller print. Look for the large word nearest to the one you are looking for first of all.

   Some Practice

   Here is a simple exercise you can try yourself to speed up your dictionary hunting.

   Write down the number of the page in your dictionary where you would find the following words. Time yourself. Remember to use those large words at the top to help you. This is a mixture of French and English words. Remember to go to the correct section and to make use of the words at the top of the page.

harbour
cochon
emploi
pocket
magasin
avis
voir
accept
vache
natation

How long did it take you? Try to improve your time. Ask someone to pick out 10 different words and try again.

2. Confusing meanings

When you look up the meaning of a French word in the dictionary you may find that there are several meanings given.

For example, if you look up the word *cuisine* you may find the following meanings

kitchen, cooking, cookery, food.

You will have to look back to your text to see which meaning is appropriate. e.g. if your text had said *Maman est dans la cuisine*, then 'kitchen' would be appropriate. On the other hand if it had said *J'adore la cuisine francaise*, then 'cooking' or 'cookery' or 'food' would be appropriate.

BE CAREFUL!!

3. Looking at individual entries

When you find the word you are looking for the dictionary entry might seem a little confusing. Let us look at one to see if I can be of some help to you.

    ①   ②   ③   ④
maison [mɛzɔ̃] *nf* house, household; ~ **de campagne**, country house;
        à la ~, at home.

①   Square brackets you ignore. They contain phonetic spelling of the word — that is how it is pronounced.

35

② *nf* tells you it is a noun *(n)* and it is feminine *(f)* (so it is *la maison*).

Other abbreviations you might find are

m — masculine; *a* — adjective; *vb*, *vt* or *vi* — a verb;
ad — adverb; *sg* — singular; *pl* — plural.

③ these are the main meanings of the word — choose carefully. Try to identify the one which is most suitable for the text you are reading.

④ this represents the word itself and simply saves room having to repeat it all the time. It is used for phrases containing that word. So ~ *de campagne* really represents *maison de campagne*, and *à la* ~ represents *à la maison*.

4. French verbs

When you look up a verb you will have to find the infinitive. For example, you will not find *je joue* you will find *jouer*, you won't find *je voudrais* but *vouloir* and so on.

5. English—French

When working from English to French be particularly cautious. If you are given several possible French words then check each one in the French to English section to get a better idea of the meaning of each one.

6. English Verbs

Remember that if you look up a verb you will find the French infinitive (e.g. *faire, regarder*). You then have to work out which person and tense of that verb to use. (Some dictionaries also have a grammar section which would help you work out the correct part.)

7. Faites attention

Above all be careful not to over-use your dictionary by looking up unimportant words or words you can easily work out. Use it carefully. If you take time to learn how to use it properly it will be a great help—if not, remember misusing a dictionary can seriously damage your French.

CHAPTER VII

READING IN STANDARD GRADE FRENCH

Reading will be assessed at all three levels. All items should be 'authentic', that is 'real' French and not specially written for the exam. You will be asked to extract information from these items in different ways.

Foundation

Items at Foundation will be very short, ranging from perhaps as little as 1, 2 or 3 words to a few sentences. Here are some examples with questions and answers.

1. You are looking for some places. You see signs (in a Town).

PISCINE MUNICIPALE	MARCHÉ COUVERT	CENTRE SPORTIF

Which of the following is not shown?

☐ Swimming Pool
☑ Town Hall
☐ Sports Centre
☐ Market   (1)

2. There is some more information below.

FERMÉ LE LUNDI
ENTRÉE: Adulte   10 Francs
                Enfant   5 Francs

Q. Today is Tuesday. Is it open?
A. Yes, (it closes on Mondays).   (1)

Q. How much is it for children to get in?
A. 5 francs.   (1)

Your penpal has left you a note.

> Je suis allé chez
> ma grand'mere.
> Elle est malade.
>
> Je reviens à sept
> heures.

Q. Where has your friend gone?
A. To his / her grandmother's house. (1)

Q. Why has she / he gone there?
A. Grandmother is ill. (1)

Q. When will he / she return?
A. At 7 o'clock. (1)

General

The items at General level will be longer than at Foundation. They will probably consist of short passages, notes, etc., of fairly straightforward French. Here is an example.

You see this article in a magazine.

LA CIGARETTE
SANS FUMÉE

La derniere invention pour les fumeurs est arrivée; la cigarette sans fumée! Oui, sans blague! Une marque americaine a mis au point une cigarette qui contient une capsule de nicotine. Plus la peine d'allumer; en aspirant, on fume, mais sans gêner les voisins.

Q. What is most unusual about this cigarette?
A. Don't have to light it. No smoke from it. (2)

Q. How did the manufacturers make this unusual cigarette?
A. Put a nicotine capsule inside. (1)

Q. What is the advantage for other people?
A. Not bothered by the smoke. (1)

Credit

At Credit level the items will consist of extended passages containing fairly complex language. Here is an example.

You find this article in a French newspaper.

HALTE AUX EXPÉRIENCES SUR LES ANIMAUX

Sept millions d'animaux son utilisés chaque année en France pour faire des recherchés sur les maladies et pour mettre au point de nouveaux médicaments. Ces expériences permettent de sauver ensuite des millions de gens, mais elles sont très choquantes car elles font souffrir des animaux. L'hôpital de Pontchaillou, à Rennes a trouvé une meilleure solution; ils ont découvert qu'on pouvait tester les nouveaux médicaments sur des cellules de foies humains, prélevées sur des volontaires durant les opérations.

This is an article about experiments on animals.

Q.1. What is the purpose of these experiments?   (2)
A.1. Research into diseases.
Test out new medicines.

Q.2. What arguments are there — for and against these experiments?   (2)
A.2. Save lives.
Animals suffer.

Q.3. What alternative has been found?   (2)
A.3. Test medicine on cells from human livers, taken from volunteers during operations.

Some Advice when Tackling Reading Items

1. Read the short introduction to each item. It will often give you some valuable information.

2. Read through the whole text, then all the questions.

3. Underline or note down any words you think might be important and whose meaning you don't know. Find these words in your dictionary.

4. Look carefully at what each question is asking and how many points are being awarded to it.

5. Don't translate big chunks of the text — look for the points relevant to the question.

6. Don't put in any more points than the question asks for — you may be penalised.

The questions in Standard Grade French Reading can take many different forms. Here are some possibilities.

True or false.
Labelling a diagram.
Ticking correct or incorrect answers from a list.
Completing a grid.
Making a choice (e.g. which restaurant to go to).
Give your own reaction (e.g. would you like this film? Why?).
Straightforward questions (who, what, when, etc.).

Later in this book there is a section containing sample Reading questions which should help you to understand what will be demanded of you in the examination.

CHAPTER VIII

SOME USEFUL LANGUAGE

As I have already strongly advised you, it is essential that you carefully organise your work in French. I would recommend that you divide your notebook or folder into 'topic' areas, such as Talking about self/family, school, shopping, leisure, holidays, etc. You should then try to build up a bank of useful language which you could use in each situation. For each topic you could also include any relevant reading materials and pieces of written work on that topic. If you work hard at developing this resource bank you will find preparation for the Speaking test much easier.

In an earlier chapter I showed you how to build up a bank of useful language for the topic of leisure. It would not of course be possible to do so for all the topics in Standard Grade French within this little book, but I will list within this section some language which you should find useful for certain topics. You could perhaps use it as a starting point for your own notebook and later develop the topics further and add on others yourself. You will find a well kept notebook or folder covering all the topics of Standard Grade French an extremely useful resource.

1. Talking about yourself

Je m'appelle . . . — My name is . . .
J'ai . . . ans. — I am . . . years old.
Dans ma famille nous sommes . . . — In my family there are . . . of us.
J'habite à (Dundee). — I live in (Dundee).
Mon anniversaire c'est le . . . — My birthday is . . .
J'ai . . . frères / soeurs. — I have . . . brothers /sisters.
Je suis enfant(e) unique. — I am an only child.
Je suis sportif (sportive). — I am sporty.
Je suis paresseux (paresseuse). — I am lazy.
Mon père est plombier. — My father is a plumber.
Mon père travaille dans un bureau. — My father works in an office.
Mon père est chomeur. — My father is unemployed.
Ma mère est institutrice. — My mother is a primary teacher.

This topic can be further developed by using the language from the topic of leisure presented earlier in this book (Chapter II, page 7).

41

2. Home / Daily Routine

J'habite une maison / un apartement. — I live in a house / a flat.

Il y a ... pièces. — There are ... rooms.

Il y a une salle de séjour. — There is a lounge.

Il y a une cuisine. — There is a kitchen.

Il y a une salle de bain. — There is a bathroom.

Il y a ... chambres. — There are ... bedrooms.

J'ai une chambre à moi. — I have my own bedroom.

Je partage une chambre avec mon frère / ma soeur.
I share a bedroom with my brother / my sister.

La maison est grande / petite / moderne / vieille.
The house is big / small / modern / old.

Tous les jours. — Every day.

Chaque matin. — Every morning.

En semaine. — During the week.

Pendant le weekend. — At the weekend.

Je me lève à ... heures. — I get up at ... o'clock.

Je m'habille. — I get dressed.

Je me lave (les cheveux). — I wash (my hair).

Je me brosse les dents. — I brush my teeth.

Pour le petit déjéuner je prends ... — For breakfast I have ...

Je quitte la maison à ... — I leave the house at ...

Je retourne chez moi à ... — I come back home at ...

Je prends le diner à ... — I have dinner at ...

Normalment on mange ... — Usually we have ...

Je me couche à ... — I go to bed at ...

Pour aider à la maison. — To help out at home.

Je fais des travaux ménagers. — I do some housework.

Je range ma chambre. — I tidy my room.

Je fais la vaiselle. — I do the dishes.

3. School / Future Career

les matières — the subjects.

le français — French.

l'anglais — English.

les maths — mathematics.

la géo(graphie) — geography.

l'histoire — history.

les sciences — science.

les travaux manuels — technical subjects.

les arts ménagers — home economics.
le dessin — art.
l'informatique — computing.

Ma matière préférée c'est . . . — My favourite subject is . . .
J'aime (bien / très bien). — I like (a lot / very much).
Je n'aime pas (tellement / du tout). — I don't like (very much / at all).
J'adore / je déteste. — I love / I hate.
Je trouve que c'est ennuyeux. — I find it is boring.
Je trouve qu c'est intéressant. — I find it is interesting.
Je trouve que c'est facile / dificile. — I find it is easy / difficult.
Je pense que c'est utile / inutile. — I think it is useful / not useful.
Je suis fort(e) . . . maths. — I am good at maths.
Je suis nul (nulle) en géo. — I am hopeless at geography.
Je ne brille pas en anglais. — I am not very good at English.
Le prof de français est sympa. — The French teacher is nice.
Le prof d'anglais est sévère. — The English teacher is strict.
Il faut travailler avec lui. — You have to work with him.
Quand je quitterai l'école je voudrais devenir (architect). —
         When I leave school I would like to be (an architect).
Je compte continuer mes etudes (à l'université). —
         I plan to continue studying (at university).
Je pense trouver un boulot. — I think I will find a job.
J'ai l'intention de me spécialiser en . . . — I intend to specialise in . . .
Je voudrais travailler en quelque chose qui concerne (les enfants). —
         I would like to work in something which concerns (children).
L'idée de devenir . . . m'attire. —
         The idea of becoming a . . . appeals to me.

4. **Holidays / Travel / Places**

l'année dernière — last year.
l'année prochaine — next year.
cette année — this year.
cet été — this summer.
j'ai passé les vacances en Espagne. — I spent my holidays in Spain.
Je vais passer les vacances à Paris. —
         I am going to spend my holiday in Paris.
J'ai passé les vacances en famille. — I went on holiday with my family.
Je vais avec des copains. — I am going with some friends.

On est allés en groupe scolaire. — We went with a school group.
On a voyagé en avoin / en voiture. — We went by plane / car.
Je vais voyager en car / en bateau. — I will travel by bus / boat.
C'était formidable / extra. — It was great / brilliant.
Je suis allé à (Versailles). — I went to (Versailles).
On a visité des monuments. — We visited monuments.
J'ai acheté des souvenirs. — I bought some souvenirs.
On a fait des excursions. — We went on some excursions.
J'ai passé le temps à (me baigner). — I spent the time (swimming).
Je vais aller à . . . — I am going to go to . . .
On a visiter . . . — We are going to visit . . .
Je vais passer le temps à (me bronzer). —
                    I will spend the time (sunbathing).
On a logé dans un hotel. — We stayed in a hotel.
On va loger dans un appartement. — We will stay in an apartment.
On a fait du camping. — We went camping.
À Paris il y a (des monuments). — In Paris there are (monuments).
Là, on peut visiter la musée. — You can visit the museum there.
On peut nager dans la mer. — You can swim in the sea.
Il y a beaucoup de distractions. — There is lots to do.
C'est une grande ville. — It's a big town.
C'est un joli petit village. — It's a pretty little village.
Qu'est-ce qu'il y a à . . .? — What is there in . . .?
Qu'est-ce qu'on peut faire / voir? — What can you see / do?
On peut (fair de l'équitation)? — Can one (go horse riding)?

5.   **Buying Things**

Avez vous? — Do you have?
Je voudrais. — I would like.
Donnez-moi . . . s'il vous plait. — Give me. . . please.
C'est combien? — How much is it?
C'est tout. — That's all.
Avez-vous quelque chose de moins cher? — Have you anything cheaper?
Est-ce que je peux le voir? — Can I see it?
Est-ce que je peux l'essayer? — Can I try it on?
C'est trop cher / grand / petit. — It's too dear / big / small.
Vous désirez? — What would you like?

6. Booking In

Avez vous une chambre de libre? — Do you have a free room?

Avez vous un emplacement de libre? — Do you have a free pitch?

C'est pour combien de personnes? — How many is it for?

Nous sommes (quatre). — There are four of us.

C'est pour combien de nuits? — How many nights is it for?

C'est pour cinq nuits. — It's for five nights.

C'est combien par nuit? — How much is it per night?

Je voudrais une chambre avec douche. —
> I would like a room with a shower.

Je voudrais une chambre avec un grand lit. —
> I would like a room with a double bed.

Je voudrais un emplacement près du bloc sanitaire. —
> I would like a pitch near the toilet block.

Le petit déjeuner est compris? — Is breakfast included?

On sert le petit déjeuner à quelle heure? — What time is breakfast?

Où se trouve la salle à manger? — Where is the dining room?

7. Making Arrangements

Tu veux sortir ce soir? — Do you want to go out tonight?

Qu'est-ce qu'on va faire? — What will we do?

Qu'est-ce que tu veux faire? — What do you want to do?

Où veux-tu aller? — Where do you want to go?

J'ai envie de . . . — I fancy . . .

Moi, je veux . . . — I want to . . .

Je pensais . . . — I was thinking of . . .

Rester à la maison. — Stay at home.

Sortir au café. — Go out to the café.

Voir un film. — See a film.

Aller au match. — Go to the match.

Tu viens avec moi? — Are you coming with me?

Moi, je préfère aller en ville. — I prefer to go into town.

Où est-ce qu'on se rencontre? — Where shall we meet?

Alors, rendez-vous au café. — We'll meet at the café.

On se rencontre à quelle heure? — At what time shall we meet?

Ça commence à quelle heure? — What time does it begin?

Ça commence à 8 heures. — It starts at 8.

Ça coute combien? — How much does it cost?

Comment est-ce qu'on y va? — How shall we get there?

On va prendre le bus / le train. — We'll catch the bus / train.

8. Reporting Lost Property

Je ne trouve pas . . . — I can't find . . .
J'ai perdu . . . — I've lost . . .
J'ai laissé . . . — I've left . . .
. . . dans le bus. — . . . in the bus.
Tu as vu? (Vous avez vu?) — Have you seen?
Tu as trouvé? (Vous avez trouvé?) — Have you found?
Je l'ai perdu ce matin. — I lost it this morning.
Je l'ai perdu hier. — I lost it yesterday.
C'est rouge / grand. — It is red / big.
C'est en cuir. — It is leather.
Il contenait . . . — It contained . . .

The language given for the topics above is not meant to be a complete list. Although many topic areas are covered, there still remain others to be tackled and all of them need to be expanded. The intention is to help you get yourself organised and to keep your own detailed file or notebook of topics and appropriate language. Remember that many topics overlap, for example, you will find that expressions of liking / disliking could occur in almost every single one. Remember too that you should keep your grammar file up to date as well so that you can make maximum use of the language you learn.

CHAPTER IX

EXAMINATION PRACTICE

This section is intended to provide examination practice for students studying for S.C.E. Standard Grade examinations in French. Three of the four examination skills are covered, i.e. Speaking, Reading and Writing. Examples in Speaking and Reading are intended to cover all three levels of Foundation, General and Credit. In Writing, only General and Credit are offered in line with S.Q.A. practice.

This practice section should be seen as a follow up to the previous sections of the book which give general advice on preparation for Standard Grade French.

The Reading items have been graded as Foundation, General and Credit. It should be noted that such gradings can only be approximate as it is not always possible to identify with complete accuracy into which level an item should fall.

The Speaking tests apply to all three levels of Foundation, General and Credit.

Suggested answers are provided for the Reading items.

SAMPLE READING ITEMS

FOUNDATION LEVEL

1. On arrival at a French campsite you see these signs.

PISCINE	DOUCHES	SALLE DE JEUX
ACCEUIL	PETANQUE	CRÊPERIE

Which of the following facilities does the site offer. Tick the appropriate ones.

Games Room	
Shop	
Showers	
Bowls	
Beach	
Tennis Courts	

3

2. You spot this poster advertising a circus.

TIGRES ELEPHANTS SINGES
CLOWNS

ICI A VOTRE CAMPING

VENDREDI A 8 h.

ENTRÉE — Adultes 40 francs
Enfants 30 francs
(moins de 10 ans)

48

(a) Where will it take place?

_____ 1

(b) When will it take place?

_____ 1

(c) How much will it cost you?

_____ 1

3. Your family wishes to make plans for the next few days. You make use of these advertisements to decide what to do.

1.

2.

3.

4.

CHEOPS ☆☆☆
HOTEL-RESTAURANT

55 chambres - Avec vue sur le château ou la campagne.
Restaurant avec ses spécialités Régionales
Service terrasse - Bar - Glacier
A proximité : Tennis - Piscine - Mini-Golf - Palais des Congrès

Centre St-Jacques - **37500 CHINON**
Tél. 47.98.46.46 - TELEX 752 547

5.

Restaurant Grill - Pizzeria

LA VILLA D'ESTE

**PIZZA
GRILLADES
ET GRATINS
AU FEU DE BOIS**
TOUS LES MIDIS
PLAT DU JOUR
1 ENTRÉE
POISSON OU
VIANDE GARNIE
DESSERT
1/4 VIN

60 F tout compris

126, rue Colbert - TOURS
Tél. 47.47.14.25

Ouvert midi et soir
Dernier service 23 h
- Fermé le dimanche -

6.

le Relais de Touraine

Hôtel*** Restaurant
**La Bodinière - RN 10
37250 VEIGNÉ**
Tél. 47.26.06.57/47.26.04.58

*A 10 mn de TOURS, le Relais de Touraine, se présente dans la
verdure et le calme de son parc boisé.
La cuisine gastronomique du restaurant se compose partic-
ulièrement de spécialités régionales traditionnelles.
Ambiance intime et reposante au bar et au salon de télévision..*

PARKING privé - A proximité : TENNIS et PISCINE

7.

DÉGUSTATIONS Vins de VOUVRAY
et de Touraine
**Domaine Claude VILLAIN
ST-Georges Rochecordon
37210 VOUVRAY** **VENTES**

Faites vos achats chez le producteur, c'est une garantie d'origine !
Exigez l'étiquette "Propriétaire-récoltant"
Tél. 47.52.50.72

Marks

Write down the number of the advert which would help if you wanted to:

(a) Try horse-riding.

_____ 1

(b) Try some sea-food dishes.

_____ 1

(c) Have a typical meal of the area in pleasant surroundings in the country.

_____ 1

(d) Have a drink in a bar overlooking the castle.

_____ 1

(e) Taste the local wine.

_____ 1

4. You are in Deauville and pick up this leaflet for a campsite.

La Campagne au bord de la Mer
à 5 km de Deauville

Piscine - Tennis
Pêche à la Truite
Terrain de Jeux
Animation - Soirée
Bibliothèque

LOCATIONS
Caravanes - Mobil-Homes
Chalets
(Semaine - Week-end)

Bar - Restaurant
Épicerie
Plats cuisinés à emporter
Pension - 1/2 Pension

(a) How far away is it?

_____ **1**

(b) Which of the following facilities does it offer?

Fishing			Caravans for Hire	
Golf			Butcher's shop	
Evening Entertainment			Discotheque	
Play Area			Take-away Food	

5

5.

ENTREE GRATUITE
VASTE PARKING GRATUIT

4–5 AOÛT 90

SA CELEBRE
FOIRE
et ses fameuses
COURSES à
ANES

SAVONNIERES
Route de Villandry   Près de TOURS

GRAND FEU D'ARTIFICE
LE DIMANCHE SOIR 5 AOÛT
Animations diverses   Groupes folkloriques

(a) On what dates will the above events take place?

_____ 1

(b) When will you have to go if you wish to see fireworks?

_____ 1

(c) List two other events taking place.

_____

_____

_____ 2

(d) Your dad wants to know if there will be a problem about parking. What can you tell him?

_____

_____ 2

6. In the campsite you are staying at, your brother wishes to join the activities club for young people.

First of all he has to fill in this form.

Write beside each section, **in English**, the information he should write down.

NOM ....

NATIONALITÉ ....

DATE DE NAISSANCE ....

SAIS-TU NAGER? ....

QUELS SONT TES INTÉRÊTS? (4 choses) ....

....

....

....

5

7. When parking the car your father had to obtain this ticket from a nearby machine.

PRIX PAYE	SEMAINE	JOUR	FIN DU STATIONNEMENT AUTORISE
01.50	28	ME	14:50

PLACER CE TICKET DERRIERE VOTRE PARE-BRISE LISIBLE DE L'EXTERIEUR

Schlumberger

(a) Until what time can the car be left?

_____   **1**

(b) Where should this ticket be left?

_____   **1**

8. You found this quiz inside a packet of sweets.

Your little brother has matched the sports to drawings as follows:

① Football   ④ Tir a l'arc
② Escrime   ⑤ Tennis
③ Course à pied   ⑥ Aviron

How many does he have correct?

_____ **1**

9.

Your father can work out that this sign refers to roadworks but does not know what it wants motorists to do.

Explain what it asks them to do.

_____

_____ **2**

10. Inside a large supermarket you see the following signs.

1. | PÂTISSERIE |

2. | CAISSE |

3. | POISSONNERIE |

4. | LÉGUMES |

5. | FROMAGES |

6. | VIANDES |

Which sign would you head for

(a) To buy carrots and onions? _____ 1

(b) To buy steak? _____ 1

(c) To pay for your shopping? _____ 1

11.

CHATEAU DE CHINON

RENSEIGNEMENTS

Téléphone : 47.93.13.45

DATES ET HEURES DE VISITES :

Du 15 mars au 30 avril :
tous les jours de 9 h à 12 h et 14 h à 18 h.

Du 1er mai au 30 juin et du 1er au 30 septembre.
tous les jours de 9 h à 18 h.

Du 1er juillet au 31 août :
tous les jours de 9 h à 19h.

Du 1er october au 14 mars:
de 9 h à 12 h et de 14 h à 17 h.

Fermé en décembre et janivier.

You arrive in Chinon on July 28th at 1 p.m.

(a) Will you be able to visit the castle straight away?

Yes ☐   No ☐   1

(b) At what time of year is the castle closed?

_____ 1

SAMPLE READING ITEMS

GENERAL LEVEL

1. This advertisement for canoe hire looks interesting.

Location tous les jours, du 1er Juillet au 31 Août. Location de Canoes et de Kayaks de 13 h à 18 h.

Tarif : 30 F/heure par personne (pour les groupes prévenir à l'avance, tarif réduit).
Matériel fourni : embarcations, gilets de sauvetage et pagaies.
Renseignements : Mr Michel Verdier tel: 47.45.37.59 ou "LA PLAGE" tel: 47.45.40.85

(a) On which days is it possible to hire a canoe?

_____ 1

(b) Why would it be better to go in a group?

_____ 1

(c) In addition to the canoe what other equipment is provided?

_____ 2

2. While in the Pyrénées you plan to visit this zoo.

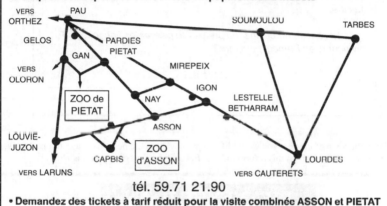

A 10 km de Pau, face aux Pyrénées
PARC ZOOLOGIQUE
NOTRE-DAME DE PIÉTAT
Le Zoo
sympa avec ses
animaux en liberté

Dans le site magnifique de la colline du Sanctuaire Notre Dame de Piétat, qui offre un panorama unique sur la chaîne des Pyrénées.
Vous pourrez admirer de très nombreuses espèces d'oiseaux et d'animaux exotiques ainsi que des collections de papillons et d'insects

VERS ORTHEZ · PAU · SOUMOULOU · TARBES · GELOS · PARDIES PIETAT · GAN · MIREPEIX · VERS OLORON · IGON · ZOO de PIETAT · NAY · LESTELLE BETHARRAM · ASSON · LOUVIE-JUZON · ZOO d'ASSON · CAPBIS · LOURDES · VERS LARUNS · VERS CAUTERETS

tél. 59.71 21.90
• Demandez des tickets à tarif réduit pour la visite combinée ASSON et PIETAT

Indicate whether the following statements are true or false.

(a) It is 15 kilometres from Pau.

      True ☐   False ☐   1

(b) The animals roam around free.

      True ☐   False ☐   1

(c) There is a great view of the city of Pau.

      True ☐   False ☐   1

(d) You will be able to see butterflies.

      True ☐   False ☐   1

3. You receive the following letter from a French friend you met on holiday.
Compose a reply to it **in English**, being careful to provide any information asked for.

Quimper, 6 juillet

Salut,

T'es bien arrivé chez toi? C'était comment le voyage? J'ai gardé un bon souvenir des vacances. On s'est bien amusés ensemble, n'est-ce pas?

Dis-moi, qu'est-ce que tu fais normalment pendant le weekend? Moi j'aime bien sortir avec mes copains. D'habitude on va au café.

Et l'année prochaine, où penses-tu passer les vacances? Tu reviendras en France, peut être?

A bientôt

Jean

4

---

4. While in the town of Poitiers you would like to pay a visit to the new space age fun park called Futuroscope. You are given this information leaflet and use it to plan your visit.

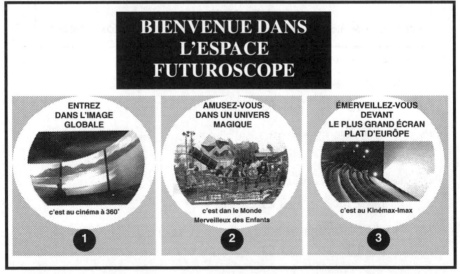

BIENVENUE DANS L'ESPACE FUTUROSCOPE

ENTREZ DANS L'IMAGE GLOBALE

c'est au cinéma à 360°

1

AMUSEZ-VOUS DANS UN UNIVERS MAGIQUE

c'est dan le Monde Merveilleux des Enfants

2

ÉMERVEILLEZ-VOUS DEVANT LE PLUS GRAND ÉCRAN PLAT D'EURÔPE

c'est au Kinémax-Imax

3

All of the attractions are numbered.
Write down the number of the attraction where you could do the following.

(a) Walk across a droplet of water _____ 1

(b) Experience a galactic adventure _____ 1

(c) Find out about the history of communication _____ 1

(d) View the park from a high point _____ 1

(e) Have a meal _____ 1

5. You also find in the leaflet some more detailed information.

Choisissez vous-même l'ordre dans lequel vous souhaitez découvrir les différents spectacles:

① Le cinéma à 360°:
Le premier cinéma circulaire d'Europe: le spectateur est encercié par une image globale produite par 9 projecteurs ... un effet saisissant!

② Le Monde Merveilleux des Enfants:
Deux hectares d'équipement de plein-air, 70 attractions dans un décor digne d'Alice au Pays des Merveilles: bateaux tamponneurs, voitures télécommandées, jeux de filets, toboggans, espace PHILIPS axé sur la découverte, maquettes LEGO retraçant l'histoire de la conquête de l'espace ... etc.

③ Le Kinémax — Salle Imax:
L'écran plat le plus grand d'Europe: 10 fois plus grand que dans une salle de cinéma classique! Vous y admiré un film unique tourné en 70 mm.

④ Le Cinéma Dynamique:
Un spectacle inoubliable: votre fauteuil bouge au gré du thème de l'image si bien que vous vous croyez vous-même au volant d'une voiture lancée à 200 km/heure ou entraîné dans une course folle sur un grand huit!

⑤ Le Pavillon du FUTUROSCOPE:
- Christophe Colomb vous entraîne dans un voyage fantastique à travers les galaxies.
- L'Exposition IBM vous offre un spectacle audiovisuel retraçant l'histoire du traitement de l'information.
- Les BANQUES POPULAIRES vous invitent à tester vos connaissances en vous amusant à dialoguer avec des ordinateurs parlants!

⑥ Les Restaurants:
Pique-nique, plateaux repas, self, restaurants (familial au gastronomique) à vous de choisir ... toujours au plus juste prix!
- La Buffeteria (à partir de 40 F).
- Le Futuroscope (32 F enfants — 45 F adolescents — 65 F adultes).
- Le Terroir (6 menus à 65 F et 75 F).
- L'Europe (menus échelonnés de 75 F à 135 F).
- Le Cristal (cuisine gastronomique avec menus).

⑦ La Gyrotour:
Admirez à 45 mètres d'altitude une architecture unique au monde: celle du Parc du FUTUROSCOPE dont l'histoire vous est révélée par un commentaire.

⑧ Promenade à travers une goutte d'eau:
A l'entrée du Pavillon de la Communication, laissez-vous entraîner dans une expérience féerique riche en sensations sonores et visuelles.
Thème central: l'eau et son fabuleux pouvoir d'évocation.

9 L'Histoire de la Communication:

Du tam-tam au satellite, l'histoire de la communication est retracée au cours d'un spectacle audoivisuel unique au monde piloté par ordinateur et projeté sur 10 écrans do toutes formes

10 Le Showscan:

Un cinéma où les images défilent à 60 images par seconde (au lieu de 24 images par seconde dans les salles traditionnelles). Résultat: une incroyable impression de réalité pour ce film inédit d'une durée d'une demi-heure.

11 Le Cinéma en Relief:

Un effet de relief comme vous n'en avez jamais vu. Les personnages viennent à vous jusqu'au milieu de la salle. Ecran et salle ne font plus qu'un dans une féerie d'images envoûtantes.

12 La Salle Omnimax:

Une nouveauté 90: un film unique à contempler sur une demicphère placée au-dessus de votre tête!

4 hôtels pour prolonger la visite:

400 chambres toutes catégories sont mises à la disposition des visiteurs:
- Centre d'hébergement du FUTUROSCOPE — (1 étoile).
- Hôtel Delta Sun — (2 étoiles) avec piscine.
- Hôtel d'Angleterre — (3 étoiles).
- Hôtel Altéa FUTUROSCOPE — (3 étoiles) avec piscine.

Marks

You have been keeping a diary of your holiday and decide to write about your visit to Futuroscope.
In your diary write (**in English**) about the **three** attractions you enjoyed most. The first one is provided as an example.

Example: *Went to the Kinema Imax — it has the biggest screen in Europe*

1. _____

2. _____

3. _____

4

6. Your penfriend's little brother has written this poem for his school magazine and shows it to you first of all.

dilling.
dilling

La cour

Les murs dégoulinants de peinture
Les arbres avec leur tronc entouré de verdure,
Les fenêtres des classes
Qui se lassent
De renvoyer les rayons du soleil, la poubelle
Pleine
De papiers de bonbons,
De marrons,
Les enfants qui crient,
Qui pleurent, qui rient,
Mais tout d'un coup, comme un malheur,
La récréation meurt
Assassinée
Par la sonnette frappée

Clément Lescat

You decide to copy it for your own school magazine and write an explanation to go with it. Explain below briefly what the poem is about. Mention where and when it takes place, what she sees and hears and what happens at the end.

_____

_____

_____

_____

_____

4

7. You come across some interesting short articles in a magazine.

280 KILOS À PERDRE!

L'homme le plus gros du monde a décidé de maigrir! Cela fait dix-sept ans que l'Américain Walter Hudson (365 kilos) est immobilisé chez lui, car ses jambes ne peuvent pas le porter! Son régime lui a déjà fait perdre 90 kilos en quatre mois. Il voudrait arriver à peser 85 kilos, ce qui lui prendra trois ans de traitement dans une clinique spécialisée.

Explain what this article is all about.

_____

_____

_____

_____

4

8.

L'ORDINATEUR
DE DEMAIN

Plus besoin de savoir taper à la machine pour travailler sur un ordinateur: deux savants américains ont inventé un appareil capable de déchiffrer l'écriture! Il suffit d'écrire une fois sur une tablette reliée à l'ordinateur les lettres de l'alphabet et les signes mathématiques qu'on utilisera. Tout est enregistré. L'ordinateur reconnaîtra très bien ensuite l'écriture sur la tablette!

What is so different about this computer?

_____

_____

_____

_____

3

9. Marie has written this letter to a magazine.

(a)

> Je suis seule avec mon père et mon frère
> parce que ma mère va accoucher.
> Nous avons tout préparé pour la petite soeur
> (nous savons déjà que c'est une petite soeur).
> Peux-tu faire une petite histoire pour les enfants
> qui sont dans le même cas que moi et aussi
> me donner des renseignements?
>
> Marie

What special event does she write about?

_____   1

(b) What information does she know already?

_____   1

(c) What does she ask the magazine to do?

_____   2

10.

GENDARMES EN CARTON

A Bremen (en Allemagne de l'Ouest), pour diminuer le nombre d'accidents de voitures provoqués par le non-respect du code de la route, le maire a fait installer des faux gendarmes en carton aux endroits les plus dangereux. Et ça marche (pour l'instant)!

Your father thinks this article about cardboard policemen must be a joke. Do you agree? Say why.

_____
_____
_____
_____   3

11. You would like to buy these magic pens for your little sister.

MAGIQUE, LE MARQUEUR!

Joue à l'agent secret avec ces deux stylos feutres! Avec le bleu, tu écris un message qui s'efface en une seconde. Avec le blanc, tu fais réapparaître ton message pendant deux minutes, puis il s'efface de nouveau! Marqueur HULA-HOOP, 30 france. En vente dans les librairies, papeteries, Prisunic.

LE FEUTRE MAGIQUE A ENCRE INVISIBLE

How do they work?

_____

_____

_____

3

12. There is a choice of films on TV tonight.

CANAL

Film

20.30   La Porte en face

Rediffusion les 11 et 17/7/90.
Téléfilm de Max Fischer.
DISTRIBUTION : George SEGAL (Jimmy Skinner), Irène CARA (Jane Flores), Clark JOHNSON (Michael), Nicholas CAMPBELL.

L'HISTOIRE —

Jimmy, à l'approche de la cinquantaine, a du mal à joindre les deux bouts. Un jour, excédé par le bruit, il se querelle violemment avec un de ses voisins. Il sort un couteau et le tue malencontreusement. Fouillant sa victime, il s'empare d'une forte somme d'argent et se terre dans son appartement. C'est un ami du mort qui est soupçonné. Une jeune femme, Jane, convaincue de son innocence, mène l'enquête et ne tarde pas à deviner la vérité.

TF1

20.30   Vampire ...
vous avez dit vampire

Film américain de Tom Holland, 1985.
Durée : 1 h 43. Fantastique. (Rediffusion le 13/7/90.)
AVEC : Chris SARANDON (Jerry Dandridge), William RAGSDALE (Charley Brewster), Amanda BEARSE (Amy Peterson), Roddy McDOWALL...

L'HISTOIRE.

Charley ne manque aucun épisode de «Fright Night», le show télévisé de Peter Vincent consacré à l'épouvante. Un jour, un nouveau voisin s'installe près de chez lui. Charley aperçoit un cercueil au cours du déménagement. La mère du garçon invite le nouveau locataire chez elle. Celui-ci révèle sa véritable nature.

****

L'avis de «France-Soir»
A mi-chemin entre le rire et l'horreur, une transposition réussie du mythe des vampires dans le monde moderne. A voir.

****

(a) Your mother enjoys films involving murder and intrigue. Which film would you recommend to her?

_____   1

(b) What is the opinion of 'France-Soir' on the film on TF1?

_____   2

(c) Which of the two would you prefer?
What are you told about the story?

_____

_____   4

66

13.

DEAUVILLE

Pour un week-end, huit jours ou plus, offrez-vous *Deauville*.

A deux heures de Paris, c'est le monde de l'élégance, de la détente, un univers de luxe, une ambiance romantique.

A mois d'aimer regarder les autres s'agiter, vous participerez aux compétitions sportives, aux événements artistiques, culturels et mondains ...

Tout l'anée, il se passe quelque chose à *Deauville*.

La mer, la campagne, le casino, les courses, les sports, les villas somptueuses, les magasins de rêve, la mode, les spectacles, les congrès: c'est tout ça *Deauville*.

In a tourist information office in Paris you pick up this leaflet about Deauville.

(a) How long should it take to get there?

_____ **1**

(b) What kind of atmosphere would you expect to find?

_____ **1**

(c) List five things which might attract people to Deauville.

_____   _____

_____   _____

_____   **5**

Marks

1. This article is about a sticker which you can put on your car.

LES ENFANTS D'ABORD!

Jacques Martin, le créateur et l'animateur de "L'école des fans" d'Antenne 2 a tenu à être le premier utilisateur de l'autocollant que vous pourrez trouver dans le numéro de juillet de "Parents", en vente depuis le 21 juin. Cet autocollant, de 12 cm de diamètre, destiné à être placé à l'arrière d'une voiture, a pour but de signaler la présence d'un ou plusieurs enfants à bord du véhicule. Quand on connaît le nombre élevé d'enfants victimes d'accidents de la route (près de 50 000 selon les dernières statistiques connues) on ne peut que saluer cette heureuse initiative du magazine "Parents" qui permettra sans doute aux automobilistes, avertis par la présence de l'autocollant, de redoubler de précautions.

comme Jaques Martin: collez votre autocollant

(a) What does it advise other drivers of?

_____   1

(b) Where can you get one from?

_____   2

(c) Why does the article think it's a good idea?

_____   2

2. You come across some very good advice on First Aid in case of a road accident.

S.O.S! P.A.S!

P.A.S. Retenez bien ces initiales. C'est facile ; enregistrez dans votre mémoire la phrase «PAS : pas de panique». Aussitôt, vous pensez, dans l'ordre, à Protéger-Alerter-Secourir.

● **Protéger** du «suraccident». Pensez à allumer les feux de détresse du véhicule accidenté, à couper le contact et à serrer le frein à main. Faites signe de ralentir aux véhicules qui arrivent. S'il y a plusieurs témoins, postez une personne dans chaque sens, à 200 mètres environ, ou avant un tournant.

● **Alerter** les secours. Par téléphone, avertissez les pompiers (n° 18), la police (n° 17) ou le SAMU (n° 15). Pour faciliter leur rapidité d'intervention, soyez précis (lieu de l'accident, sens de la circulation, nombre de blessés ...). Pensez surtout à répondre clairement aux questions qu'on vous posera. Vos indications feront gagner du temps aux sauveteurs.

● **Secourir le blessé**. Observez-le et parlez-lui : c'est déjà beaucoup. Votre voix rassurera la victime et minimisera les effets de l'état de choc.

(a) What is the significance of the letters P.A.S?

_____

_____ **2**

(b) Mention three things you could do first of all.

_____

_____

_____ **3**

(c) What information should you give to the emergency services?

_____

_____

_____ **3**

(d) Why should you talk to the victim?

_____

_____ **2**

3. This article refers to some acts of hooliganism in England.

La troisième mi-temps
des hooligans anglais

■ LONDRES
De notre correspondante

Meurtre, émeutes, bagarres, scènes de pillage : l'autre nuit, plusieurs villes d'Angleterre ont été le théâtre de sérieux incidents après la défaite de l'équipe nationale face à la R.F.A., en demi-finale du Mondiale, à Turin.

Des centaines jeunes gens, amassés dans les pubs, ont déferlé dans les rues à la fin de la retransmission télévisée, brisant les vitres des maisons, pillant les magasins et lançant toutes sortes de projectiles et bouteilles de verre aux malheureux passants qui se trouvaient par hasard sur leur chemin.

Deux cents hooligans ont été arrêtés Ronald Goodwin, un électricien de 33 ans qui s'était opposé à un groups de braillards éméchés, a été frappé à mort puis abandonné dans une mare de sang, près de Southampton. Six personnes sont interrogées par la police.

A Brighton, cent cinquante étudiants allemands de passage dans la ville sont restés barricadés dans un night-club où ils s'étaient réfugiés pour échapper à la colère de près de deux cents hooligans mécontents d'avoir perdu. La police, appelée à la rescousse, a réussi à rétablir le calme peu après.

A Eltham, une petite ville au sud-est de Londres, plusieurs voitures portant des immatriculations allemandes ont été renversées. Certaines ont même été incendiées. Vingt personnes ont été arrêtées.

(a) What brought about these incidents?

_____

_____ **2**

(b) What kinds of incidents took place in general?

_____

_____ **3**

(c) Give details of two incidents reported in the article.

_____

_____

_____ **8**

4. This article appears in the sports section of a French newspaper. It is obviously about Peter Shilton, goalkeeper of the English national football team.

LE GARDIEN ANGLAIS A DÉCIDÉ DE METTRE FIN A SA CARRIÈRE INTERNATIONALE

Good bye, Mr. Shilton

Photo AP

Shilton essuie peut-être une larme. Il vient de disputer son dernier match avec l'équipe d'Angleterre.

D'un de nos envoyés spéciaux

BARI

Sans grande émotion, avec sérieux et dignité, Peter Shilton a décidé : il ne gardera plus les buts de l'équipe d'Angleterre. Samedi à Bari, il a disputé son dernier match, encaissé ses derniers buts. Agé de 40 ans, avec cent vingt-cinq sélections, Shilton passe la main: « Je quitte le football international. Mais je ne voulais pas le faire avant ce dernier match. Je l'avais dit au sélectionneur Bobby Robson. Je tenais à finir à mon meilleur niveau. Et je voulais terminer ici ma carrière. Aux jeunes de se montrer. En tout cas, je me suis bien amusé pendant vingt ans.»

Que va-t-il devenir? Il ne s'en fait pas spécialement à ce sujet : « Jusqu'à maintenant j'étais occupé par la Coupe du monde. J'ai des idées sur mon avenir mais je ne veux pas encore y penser. Je vais d'abord rentrer chez moi, après on verra. Je vais continuer avec mon club Derby County. Tant que je peux jouer en première division je continue.»

(a) What important decision has he taken?

_____

_____ 1

(b) Why has he taken this decision?

_____

_____ 2

(c) What are his plans for the future?

_____

_____ 3

5. This letter appeared in a magazine written by a young French boy who now lives in Zaire.

«MON PÈRE A ÉTÉ ARRÊTÉ

«Bonjour! Mon nom est Thomas Lumbi. Je suis né en France, et j'ai vécu cinq ans au Zaïre (Afrique centrale).

Je ne sais pas si vous êtes au courant, mais, en ce moment, au Zaïre, des révoltes éclatent. La population a souffert pendant trop d'années.

Mon père est ... Zaïrois. Il a fondé une association nommée « Solidarité Paysanne », qui, au départ, avait pour but de réunir les paysans entre eux, afin de réfléchir sur des problèmes et les résoudre.

Et, vu les circonstances au Zaïre, les autorités surveillent de près Solidarité Paysanne. Résultat : mon père et d'autres personnes one été arrêtés. Voici leurs noms : Lumbi Ohongo, Kapitaine Mavamba, T'Shibanda.

Pour que leur protection soit assurée, nous devons faire passer des informations partout, dans les journaux, aux ministres, ainsi qu'à Frères des Hommes, une organisation soutenant Solidarité Paysanne.

Pour plus d'informations, vous pouvez vous renseigner à Frères des Hommes, 45 bis, rue de la Glacière, 75013 Paris.

Tel : (1)47.07.00.00.

(a) According to Thomas, what is happening at the moment in Zaïre?

_____

_____ 1

(b) What has happened to his father and why?

_____

_____ 4

(c) Why has Thomas written this letter?

_____

_____ 2

6. A very interesting article appears in a magazine about Paul-Émile Victor, a French explorer. He is interviewed about his adventures and opinions on the environment.

PAUL-ÉMILE VICTOR

Paul-Émile Victor est le fondateur des Expéditions polaires françaises. Ce savant, mondialement connu, a fait plus de trente expéditions dans les déserts de glace de l'Arctique et de l'Antarctique. Aujourd'hui, Paul-Émile Victor a 83 ans. Il vit, avec sa femme Colette et son fils Teïva, à Bora-Bora, un îlot de Polynésie, en plein milieu de l'océan Pacifique. C'est là que Marc Beynié, reporter au *Pèlerin Magazine*, l'a recontré pour nous.

L'AVENIR DE L'ANTARCTIQUE
Marc Beynié : *Vous avez créé la première base scientifique français en Antarctique. Comment imaginez-vous l'avenir de cet immense continent?*
Paul-Émile Victor : Ma position est claire et nette : le continent antarctique doit rester un parc mondial, réservé à la recherche scientifique internationale. Un point, c'est tout!

ACTIVITÉ MILITAIRE
Marc Beynié : *Aujourd'hui, trente-neuf pays ont signé un traité qui interdit toute activité militaire en Antarctique ...*
Paul-Émile Victor : Depuis près de quarante ans, l'Antarctique est un continent de coopération internationale. Là-bas, tout marche exeptionnellement bien : des scientifiques d'une vingtaine de pays collaborent entre eux de façon totale, et sans aucune arrière-pensée. C'est un cas unique au monde. Il faut que cela continue!

LES RICHESSES
Marc Beynié : *On parle beaucoup des richesses de l'Antarctique. Existent-elles vraiment?*
Paul-Émile Victor : On a raconté beaucoup de choses fausses à leur sujet. Dites-vous qu'il y a 300 millions d'années, tous les continents étaient réunis en us seul grand continent.

À l'époque, l'Antarctique touchait l'Afrique du Sud, l'Amérique du Sud, l'Inde et l'Australie. Cette proximité laisse donc supposer la présence de minerais. Certains prétendent même qu'il y a d'énormes gisements de pétrole en Antarctique.

CHARBON ET PÉTROLE
Marc Beynié : *Pour l'instant, a-t-on trouvé quelque chose?*
Paul-Émile Victor : Pas vraiment! On a juste repéré du charbon de basse qualité, au centre de l'Antarctique. Évidemment, il coûte bien trop cher à extraire. D'ailleurs, toutes ces éventuelles richesses sont enfouies sous plusieurs milliers de mètres de glace.

Et puis, vous savez, nos réserves mondiales de pétrole, de matières premières et de métaux nous suffisent, sans doute, pour des milliers d'années.

Nous n'avons donc pas besoin des matières premières que pourrait contenir l'Antarctique!

LES POISSONS
Marc Beynié : *Il doit aussi y avoir énormément de poissons dans l'océan glacial Antarctique ...*
Paul-Émile Victor : Il y a des centaines de milliers de tonnes de « krill ». Ce sont de minuscules crevettes qui servent de nourriture aux baleines et aux phoques. Elles représentent aussi une source de protéines fantastique.

Mais, d'ici à vingt ou trent ans, on saura fabriquer les protéines atrificielles. Ce « krill » n'aura donc plus d'intérêt!

LE FROID

Marc Beynié : *Il y a quinze ans, vous avez pris votre retraite au soleil, à Bora-Bora. En aviez-vous vraiment assez du froid de l'Antarctique?*

Paul-Émile Victor : Un jour, j'ai dit, en plaisantant, que j'avais horreur de la glace et de la neige ... Mais ce n'est pas vrai! J'aime ça! J'adore ça! J'ai vécu cinquante ans dans le froid! Personne ne m'a obligé à le faire.

Vous savez, quand j'étais enfant, je voulais absolument réaliser deux choses: partir dans les régions polaires, et aller en Polynésie. Je réalise maintenant mon deuxième rêve!

RETRAITE EN POLYNÉSIE

Marc Beynié : *Qu'est-ce qui vous a attiré en Polynésie?*

Paul-Émile Victor : Ici, je vis et je travaille facilement: je ne suis pas dérangé. Si j'avais choisi de vivre dans une grande ville comme Paris, j'aurais perdu beaucoup trop de temps en déplacements. Ça, je le refuse: pour moi, le temps est le bien le plus précieux de l'homme. L'argent, non: on en gagne, on en perd, on en regagne, on s'en passe ...

La santé, ce n'est pas non plus toujours l'essentiel: on peut vivre avec des maladies, et rester actif et positif. Le temps, c'est différent. On en manque! L'homme est coincé entre la naissance et la mort.

PROTECTION DES ANIMAUX

Marc Beynié : *Aujourd'hui, on parle beaucoup de protection des animaux sauvages. Qu'en pensez-vous?*

Paul-Émile Victor : Défendre les bébés phoques, pourquoi pas? Mais je trouve qu'il y a partout dans le monde, des causes beaucoup plus importantes: des massacres et des guerres de toutes sortes, des tribus que l'on laisse mourir de faim.

Le grand effort que nous devroins tous faire, c'est de sauver les hommes en perdition.

OPTIMISME

Marc Beynié : *Notre Terre est belle, mais fragile. Saurons-nous la protéger?*

Paul-Émile Victor : À moyen terme, je suis pessimiste. Mais, à longue échéance, je reste optimiste. Pourquoi? Parce que, partout, les gouvernements se rendent compte que l'environnement est important. Ils commencent à s'en occuper sérieusement.

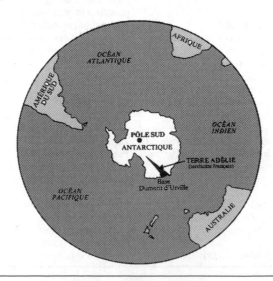

You are interested in this explorer and look through the article to find his views on **certain** matters.

(a) What does he think should be the future of Antartica?

_____

_____

_____ 2

(b) Why does he think the world should not try to extract coal and oil from Antartica?

_____

_____

_____ 3

(c) Why did he decide to go and live in Polynesia?

_____

_____

_____

_____ 2

(d) What is his opinion on the protection of wild animals?

_____

_____

_____

_____ 3

SPECIMEN SPEAKING TEST A

FOUNDATION, GENERAL and CREDIT LEVELS

CANDIDATE'S GUIDANCE FOR PREPARATION

N.B. These sample speaking tests contain five areas to give a wider range of the kind of situations you might expect to face. In the actual test you will be given only three situations.

This paper is intended to help the candidate to prepare for the Speaking test. You do not have to deal with every detail in the areas of conversation. You may introduce points of your own.

The situation you have to imagine is as follows:

> A French boy / girl has come to stay in your house on an exchange visit for a week.

(Your teacher will take the part of the young French person.)

AREA 1 — Find out about his / her family.

You could ask about:
      his / her parents and their jobs,
      brothers / sisters their names and ages,
      whether he / she has any pets,
      where they live,
and be prepared to talk about your own family.

AREA 2 — Discuss the journey he / she has just made.

You could ask about:
      How he / she travelled.
      How long the journey took.
      How he / she passed the time
      If he / she enjoyed the journey.
You might also discuss a journey you have made.

AREA 3 — Find out what he / she would like to eat / drink while staying with you.

You could:
        Discuss likes and dislikes of food and drink.
        Compare your own tastes.
        Explain what you normally have at mealtimes.
        Find out what he / she normally has in France.
        Compare Scottish and French eating habits.

AREA 4 — Discuss plans for the coming week.

You could:
        Find out his / her interests.
        Tell what your own interests are.
        Explain what places of interest there are in your area.
        Suggest some activities.

AREA 5 — Tell him / her about your school which he / she will visit tomorrow.

You could:
        Say how you are doing at school.
        Explain what subjects are offered at your school.
        Tell him / her what the teachers are like.
        Find out about his / her school.
        Discuss what to do at lunch time.

SPECIMEN SPEAKING TEST A

FOUNDATION, GENERAL and CREDIT LEVELS

CANDIDATE'S TEST PAPER

The situation you have to imagine is as follows:

>A French boy / girl has come to stay in your house on an exchange visit for a week.

AREA 1 — Find out about his / her family.

AREA 2 — Discuss the journey he / she has just made.

AREA 3 — Found out what he / she would like to eat / drink while staying with you.

AREA 4 — Discuss plans for the coming week.

AREA 5 — Tell him / her about your school which he / she will visit tomorrow.

SPECIMEN SPEAKING TEST B

FOUNDATION, GENERAL and CREDIT LEVELS

CANDIDATE'S GUIDANCE FOR PREPARATION

This paper is intended to help the candidate to prepare for the Speaking test. You do not have to deal with every detail in the areas of conversation. You may introduce points of your own.

The situation you have to imagine is as follows:

> As part of an exchange visit you are spending a week in a French school. One of the staff thinks it would be a good idea to record an interview between you and a French boy/girl of the same age, to form the basis for an article in the school magazine.

(Your teacher will take the part of the young French person.)

AREA 1 — Find out a little about each other.

You could discuss:
> Names, ages, nationality, etc.
> Family.
> Why you have come to France.
> How long you are staying for.

AREA 2 — Talk about your impressions of the town where you are staying in France.

You say:
> What you have visited so far.
> What you think of the shops/facilities, etc.
> What other things you would like to see and do.
> Compare it to your own home town.

AREA 3 — Compare school life in France and Scotland.

You could talk about:
> Starting and finishing times, days attended.
> Subjects you study.
> Likes and dislikes at school.
> Relationships with teachers.

AREA 4 — Discuss how you each spend your free time.

You might mention:
Sports and hobbies.
Television — favourite programmes.
A typical weekend.

AREA 5 — Tell him / her about Scotland.

You could mention/discuss:
The journey you had to make from Scotland
The attractions of Scotland.
The weather!
The food (does everyone eat chips all the time??).
The main differences between life in France and in Scotland.

SPECIMEN SPEAKING TEST B

FOUNDATION, GENERAL and CREDIT LEVELS

CANDIDATE'S TEST PAPER

The situation you have to imagine is as follows:

>As part of an exchange visit you are spending a week in a French school. One of the staff thinks it would be a good idea to record an interview between you and a French boy/girl of the same age, to form the basis for an article in the school magazine.

AREA 1 — Find out a little about each other.

AREA 2 — Talk about your impressions of the town where you are staying in France.

AREA 3 — Compare school life in France and in Scotland.

AREA 4 — Discuss how you each spend your free time.

AREA 5 — Tell him / her about Scotland.

SAMPLE WRITING ITEMS

GENERAL LEVEL

Test A

Your class is setting up a link with a class in a French school.

Write a few words IN FRENCH for each of the following.

1. Write a short note with your name, age and some family details.

---

2. Write a short description of yourself and mention some of the things you like doing.

Moi:

Mes passetemps:

3. Describe briefly your favourite teacher and what you like/don't like about school

Mon prof . . .

Au College . . .

4. Write down a few questions for your future pen pal to answer. Find out his / her name, age, favourite school subjects and something about hobbies / pastimes.

3. At Xmas you spend a week skiing in Aviemore. Send a postcard to your pen pal saying where you are, how you are enjoying yourself, what the accommodation is like and what you have done so far.

SAMPLE WRITING ITEMS

GENERAL LEVEL

Test B

You are spending a week at the house of your French friend, Jean-Pierre.

Write a few words IN FRENCH for each of the following.

1. It is your friend's little brother's birthday. You have brought a card with you but it is in English. You decide to write a short message in French inside.

2. You are alone at home when your friend's aunt phones to say she will arrive on Saturday at 3 p.m. and wants someone to meet her at the station. You write a note in French for Jean-Pierre's parents.

3. At your friend's school they are trying to match up groups with similar interests. Write down four sentences about the things you like and don't like to do.

Mes passetemps

---

4. You go along to Jean-Pierre's youth club. They are carrying out a survey. You are asked to fill in this form.

Nom . . . .

Nationalité . . . .

Sports préférés . . . .

. . . .

. . . .

Autres passetemps . . . .

. . . .

. . . .

. . . .

Ambition . . . .

. . . .

Musique favorite . . . .

. . . .

5. On returning home you send a short letter to Jean-Pierre telling him what the journey was like and thanking him and his family for their hospitality.

SAMPLE WRITING ITEMS

CREDIT LEVEL

Test A

LES AMIS

Below, some young French people write about their friends and what they like doing together.

Moi, j'ai beaucoup d'amis, au collège, à la maison des jeunes et plusieurs qui habitent près de chez moi. On se rencontre souvent pour aller en ville, faire du sport ou aller à la disco. J'adore être avec mes amis.

(ROGER 16)

Moi, j'ai plusieurs amis mais je ne sors pas souvent avec eux parce que je n'ai pas le temps. Cette année j'ai dû consacrer beaucoup de temps à mon travail scolaire. J'ai mes amis du collège que je vois chaque jour. On bavarde et on rit beaucoup ensemble.

(MARIE 15)

Sortir avec des amis? Bof, ça ne me dit pas grande chose. Je n'ai qu'une seule amie, Veronique. On fait du tout ensemble. On se passe des choses, les disques, les vêtements, les livres. Elle est super, Veronique.

(NATHALIE 15)

What about you?
Do you have lots of friends?
Do you have a special friend?
What about your pals at school?
What do you and your friends like doing together?

Express your ideas IN FRENCH in about 200 words.

SAMPLE WRITING ITEMS

CREDIT LEVEL

Test B

The article below is written by a French school pupil on his first day back at school.

He has mixed feelings about going back.

Will all his friends be back?

Exams coming up. A harder year ahead.

What will the teachers be like?

La rentrée

Ce matin, quand j'ai repris le chemin du collège je ne parvenais pas à me faire de souci: mes super-copains de l'année de quatrième, j'étais à peu près sûr de tous les retrouver cette année. Et côté boulot, ça n'allait plutôt pas trop mal pour moi. Alors, côôl! A la fin de l'année, les profs nous avaient pourtant bien expliqué (ils en avaient même fait des kilos!) que la troisième c'est très important . . . Pourquoi, déjà? Ah oui, à cause du passage en seconde qu'il ne faut pas rater, des options pour l'année prochaine qu'il faudra choisir, et les examens . . . En arrivant à la porte, je me posais une seule question: qui seraient nos profs?

Finalement, tout s'est très bien passé. En maths, on a le même prof que l'an passé: Marchaudon. Il me fait rire, avec ses pulls trop grands et son air rêveur, mais c'est un super-prof, très clair et très patient. En anglais, un nouveau, un certain Peter Groseille. En français, Mme Allaoui, bof! Je la déteste. Mais la bonne nouvelle, c'est le prof principal: Jean-Louis Badini, le prof de gym (pardon, d'EPS). Il m'a à la bonne: mes 11 s 9 au 100 mètres n'y sont pas pour rien. Et Virginie est à côté de moi, comme l'an dernier. L'année sera bonne, je le sens.

What about you?
Do you enjoy going back to school after the holidays?
Do you look forward to meeting your friends, tackling harder work, having new teachers, picking new subjects, doing exams?

Express your opinions IN FRENCH in about 200 words.

ANSWERS TO SAMPLE READING ITEMS

FOUNDATION LEVEL

Marks

1. Games room □; Showers □; Bowls □   **(3)**

2.   *(a)*   In the campsite.   **(1)**
     (b)   Friday at 8 p.m.   **(1)**
     (c)   40 francs.   **(1)**

3.   *(a)*   2   **(1)**
     (b)   1   **(1)**
     (c)   4   **(1)**
     (d)   3 or 4   **(1)**
     (e)   7   **(1)**

4.   *(a)*   5 kilometres   **(1)**
     (b)   Fishing □; Evening entertainment □; Play area □;
         Caravans for hire □; Take-away food □.   **(5)**

5.   *(a)*   4th/5th August.   **(1)**
     (b)   Sunday evening.   **(1)**
     (c)   (Any 2)
         A fair
         Donkey races
         Folk music.   **(2)**
     (d)   There is a huge car park.
         Parking is free.   **(2)**

6.

```
NOM .....................  Your name  ..................
NATIONALITÉ ................  Your nationality  .............
DATE DE NAISSANCE .......  Your date of birth  ...........
SAIS-TU NAGER? .............  Can you swim  ............
QUELS SONT TES INTÉRÊTS? (4 choses)  List 4 things you like doing
.................................................
.................................................
.................................................
```

7. (a) 2.50 p.m. (14.50)   (1)
    (b) Inside the windscreen.   (1)

8. 4 (fencing, archery, tennis, rowing)   (1)

9. Slow down. Be careful.   (2)

10. (a) 4   (1)
    (b) 6   (1)
    (c) 2   (1)

11. (a) Yes.   (1)
    (b) December and January.   (1)

GENERAL LEVEL

Marks

1.   *(a)*   Every day.   **(1)**
     (b)   There is a reduction.   **(1)**
     (c)   Life jackets, paddles.   **(2)**

2.   *(a)*   False.   **(1)**
     (b)   True.   **(1)**
     (c)   False.   **(1)**
     (d)   True.   **(1)**

3.   Your letter should mention the following points.
     1.   What the journey was like.
     2.   Some comment about the holiday you have just spent in France.
     3.   What you do at weekends.
     4.   Where you are going on holiday next year.   **(4)**

4.   *(a)*   8   **(1)**
     (b)   5   **(1)**
     (c)   9   **(1)**
     (d)   7   **(1)**
     (e)   6   **(1)**

5.   Sample answer — you may of course have picked different attractions.
     1.   Went to the fantastic circular cinema — surrounded by screens.
     2.   The history of communication was interesting — it was shown on 10 screens!
     3.   Walked across a droplet of water! It showed the fabulous power of water.   **(3)**

6.   This is a rather difficult item to provide answers for but you should mention the following points.
     1.   It is set in a school playground OR at interval time.   **(3)**
     2.   She mentions the things she sees OR she sees walls with peeling paint / sun reflected in windows / the dustbin full of papers and chestnuts. (**Any one item.**).   **(1)**
     3.   She mentions the noises the children make OR the children are shouting / crying / laughing. (**Any one item.**)   **(1)**
     4.   The school bells brings it all to an end OR the end of the interval.   **(1)**

7.   Any 4 of the following six points.
     It's about the fattest man in the world.
     He has decided to lose weight.
     He can't leave the house.
     His legs won't support him.
     He wants to get his weight down to 85 kilos (or lose 280 kilos).
     It will take him 3 years.   **(4)**

8. You don't have to type in information.
    It can read normal writing.
    You can write on a pad linked to the computer. **(3)**

9. *(a)* Her mother is going to have a baby. **(1)**
    (b) It is a girl. **(1)**
    (c) Publish a story for children in her situation. Give her some information. **(2)**

10. No — it's true.
    They have been placed at dangerous places
    (to prevent accidents). **(3)**

11. You write your message with the blue pen / it disappears / and is made visible with
    the white one. **(3)**

12. *(a)* La Porte en face. **(1)**
    (b) Worth seeing / mixture of comedy and horror / a modern-day version of the vampire
    theme. (**Any 2 points from 3.**) **(2)**
    (c) PORTE EN FACE: Jimmy is about 50 / has a quarrel with neighbour / kills him /
    steals a lot of money from him / a friend is suspected of the murder / Jane finds out
    the truth.
    VAMPIRE ... VOUS AVEZ DIT VAMPIRE: Charley always watches "Friday Night"
    (A horror programme) / a new neighbour moves in / Charley spots a coffin during the
    removal / Charley's mother invites the new neighbour to their house / then his real
    identity is revealed.
    It obviously depends which film you selected but score a maximum of 4 from the
    points shown above. **(2)**

13. *(a)* 2 hours. **(1)**
    (b) Romantic / elegant. **(1)**
    (c) Any 5 points from the following: sport / culture / art / fashion / sea / countryside /
    casino / racing / luxury villas / shops / shows. **(5)**

CREDIT LEVEL

Marks

1.   *(a)*   There is a child in the car.   **(1)**
   (b)   July edition of / "Parents" magazine.   **(2)**
   (c)   Many (50 000) children are victims of accidents each year / it should make drivers more cautious.   **(2)**

2.   *(a)*   It stands for **DON'T** panic / and reminds you to Protect, Alert and Comfort the victim.   **(2)**
   (b)   Put on hazard warning lights / switch off engine / put on handbrake / tell other traffic to slow down / if possible put other people on either side to warn traffic. (**Any 3 points.**).   **(3)**
   (c)   The location / direction of traffic (i.e. which side of the road) / number of injured.   **(3)**
   (d)   It will reassure him / and minimuse the effects of shock.   **(2)**

3.   *(a)*   The defeat of England by West Germany in the World Cup.
             Young people leaving pubs after watching the game on T.V.   **(2)**
   (b)   Windows broken / shops looted / missiles thrown at passers-by.   **(3)**
   (c)   There are three incidents to choose from — 4 points each.
          1.   A young electrician stood up to the hooligans / was beaten to death / left in a pool of blood / 6 arrested.
          2.   150 German students staying in Brighton / had to take refuge in a night club / to escape from 200 hooligans / police managed to restore order.
          3.   Several cars with German number plates / were overturned / some set on fire / 20 arrested.   **(8)**

4.   *(a)*   To retire from his position as England's goalkeeper (played his last match for England).   **(1)**
   (b)   Wanted to stop at the peak of his form / make way for younger players.   **(2)**
   (c)   Has some idea but will go home first and think about it / will continue with Derby County / will continue in 1st Division while he can.   **(3)**

5.   *(a)*   There have been rebellions (revolts).   **(1)**
   (b)   He has been arrested / He founded an organisation (Solidarité Paysanne) / to unite the people / to solve their problems / the authorities kept a close watch on their activities. First point plus any other 3.   **(4)**
   (c)   To publicise what has happened / to help protect them.   **(2)**

6.   *(a)*   It must remain a world reserve (park) / for scientific research.   **(2)**
   (b)   It is expensive to extract / it is buried below thousands of metres of ice / the world already has sufficient reserves elsewhere.   **(3)**
   (c)   Finds it easy to live and work there / would have wasted too much time in a city, travelling around.   **(2)**
   (d)   Not really against it / but there are other more important causes in the world / the most important thing is to protect mankind.   **(3)**

NOTES

NOTES

Printed by Bell & Bain Ltd., Glasgow, Scotland.